Navigating the High Seas of Business: A Pirate's Lesson

Navigating the High Seas of Business: A Pirate's Lesson

By Lance Harris

Copyright © 2023 Lance Harris

First paperback edition September 2023

Book design by Lance Harris
All figures and art created by Midjourney.com

ISBN 9798859283484 (paperback)
Independently published

DEDICATION

To my amazing and wonderful wife Alison
and daughter-ish Sami.
Thank you for your support and
encouragement.

TABLE OF CONTENTS

Introduction

By Captain Martin Marlinspike

Avast ye ambitious buccaneers and future captains of industry! As ye set forth on this grand expedition, be ready to master the unpredictable currents of commerce, armed with the savvy of a pirate. Tis Captain Martin Marlinspike here, your land lubber of an author asked that I be your Pirate guide on this wee adventure. I am here to regale ye with tales of audacity, wit, and cunning from the golden age of piracy, and to draw parallels with the bustling bazaars of today's business world. The world of piracy, with its legends, myths, and real-life adventurers, has always been a source of fascination These swashbucklers, often seen as outlaws, were not just seekers of fortune but also shrewd businessmen, masterful negotiators, and unparalleled leaders. Their stories, brimming with lessons on agility, innovation, and daring, echo loudly in the boardrooms of today.

As we embark on this odyssey, ye'll learn that the pirate's code, often whispered as mere guidelines, imparts wisdom on the significance of nimbleness and resilience in trade. In a world that's ever-shifting, the prowess to adapt, to innovate with audacity, and to steer one's own destiny is paramount. The zest for adventure that fueled the pirate's heart is the very essence that ignites today's moguls of industry.

Their unyielding quest for treasures, their boldness against all odds, and their fierce desire for autonomy reflect the spirit of today's entrepreneurs. It's a spirit that champions the daring, values the audacious, and celebrates the relentless chase of one's dreams.

The vast oceans, with their fickle waves and treacherous tempests, mirror the unpredictable nature of business. Pirates, those masterful helmsmen of these waters, knew that to prosper, one must be malleable, ready to alter course on a whim, and perpetually poised to innovate. Their chronicles, rich with bold ventures and ingenious tactics, light the way for today's leaders, revealing the route to triumph in the ever-evolving marketplace. As we delve deeper, ye'll grasp the core of the pirate's code and its pertinence in today's corporate seas. "The Code is More What You'd Call 'Guidelines'" will unveil the essence of approaching rules with a flexible mindset, fostering innovation and adaptability amidst the swift currents of business.

The chapters ahead will whisk ye across the vast oceans, gleaning wisdom from legendary marauders and their brazen endeavors. From the art of clear intentions in " Even pirates, before they attack another ship, hoist a black flag" to the craft of bartering and forging alliances in "Take what you can, give nothing back", each chapter will bestow insights as pertinent to the corporate suite as to a pirate's galley. "Dead Men Tell No Tales" will probe the importance of discretion, trustworthiness, and reputation in trade. Much like pirates valued the sanctity of buried treasures, today's magnates must understand the worth of discretion and its role in forging trust and authority.

Navigating these tales, ye'll also encounter real-world business sagas, drawing parallels with the stratagems and ruses of pirates. These narratives, from both the pirate's deck and the trader's desk, serve as case studies, exemplifying the ageless tenets that underpin success in any venture. Captain Martin Marlinspike's insights, harvested from his unique perch at the crossroads of piracy and commerce, will be your trusty compass. His tales, reflections, and musings will enrich the lessons gleaned from the vast oceans.

As ye traverse this tome, ye'll discern that the worlds of piracy and commerce are intertwined in their essence. The trials, the tactics, and the spirit that shape both realms are uncannily akin. It's a nod to the ageless wisdom we can extract from history, from legends, and from the chronicles of those who dared to chase the horizon. So, ready yerselves for an unparalleled voyage. With the winds favoring our journey and the boundless ocean ahead, we'll plumb the depths of buccaneer brilliance and its significance in today's bustling world of trade. It's an expedition teeming with thrill, enlightenment, and a chest full of lessons to bolster your own ventures.

Figure 1- Midjourney(2023)

As we hoist the sails, heed the words of a legendary swashbuckler: " It's not about the gold, it's about the glory." In the realm of trade, much like on the open seas, it's the voyage, the hurdles surmounted, and the legacy etched that truly count. The parallels between the world of pirates and the domain of business are profound. Both demand a certain level of audacity, a willingness to embrace risks, and the vision to see opportunities where others see challenges. Pirates, with their insatiable thirst for adventure and their relentless pursuit of freedom, epitomize the essence of what it takes to succeed in any endeavor.

Their tales, laden with audacious feats, ingenious schemes, and an indomitable spirit, stand as a testament to the might of determination, adaptability, and vision. In the realm of commerce, these very traits distinguish the pioneers from the masses, the trailblazers from the followers, and the legends from the mundane. So, raise the anchor, man the helm, and get set to journey through time, drawing lessons from the daring marauders of old and applying them to the dynamic world of commerce. May the winds be ever in your favor and may fortune smile upon you as you navigate the high seas of commerce.

Till we meet again on some distant shore, may the winds be kind and the seas be calm. Let the odyssey commence!

Chapter 1: "A Pirate's Life for Me" - Embracing the Spirit of Adventure in Business

Aaaarrrrgggghhhh!, intrepid readers! As we set sail on this grand voyage through the vast and tumultuous seas of business, it's only fitting that we begin our journey with the very essence of piracy - the spirit of adventure. The world of piracy, with its tales of daring escapades, hidden treasures, and fierce battles, has always been a source of intrigue and fascination. But beyond the buccaneer adventures and legendary tales, these pirates were more than just rebels of the seas. They were visionaries, risk-takers, and pioneers, much like today's entrepreneurs and business leaders.

In the golden age of piracy, the seas were a realm of endless possibilities and unparalleled dangers. Pirates, with their iconic black flags and fearsome reputations, ruled these waters, seeking out treasures and establishing their own codes of conduct. But what truly set them apart was their indomitable spirit of adventure. They were willing to venture into the unknown, to face insurmountable odds, and to challenge the status quo. This spirit, this relentless pursuit of the horizon, is what defines the essence of piracy. And it's this very essence that finds deep resonance in today's dynamic world of business. Just as the seas were a vast, uncharted territory for pirates, the business landscape today offers its own set of challenges, opportunities, and treasures waiting to be discovered.

Now, one might ponder, what parallels can be drawn between the swashbuckling world of pirates and the structured realm of business? The answer lies in the underlying principles that drive both worlds. At the heart of every pirate's adventure was a thirst for discovery, a hunger for riches, and a willingness to take risks. They were not bound by conventions, nor were they deterred by failures. They embraced uncertainty, charted their own paths, and carved out legends that have stood the test of time. Similarly, in the world of business, it's the trailblazers, the innovators, and the visionaries who leave an indelible mark. They venture into uncharted territories, challenge established norms, and rewrite the rules of the game.

So, as we embark on this chapter, let's channel the spirit of these legendary pirates. Let's embrace the sense of adventure, the willingness to take risks, and the drive to discover new horizons. For in the world of business, as on the high seas, it's the bold, the daring, and the audacious who truly make their mark. Join me, dear reader, as we set sail on this exciting journey, drawing inspiration from the tales of pirates, and applying their timeless wisdom to the challenges and opportunities of the modern business world.

1. The Allure of the Unknown: Venturing Beyond Safe Harbors

The vast, boundless oceans have always been a symbol of the unknown, a realm of endless possibilities and untold mysteries. For pirates, these waters represented more than just a physical expanse; they were a canvas upon which they painted their dreams, ambitions, and desires. Every horizon held the promise of a new adventure, every uncharted island was a potential treasure trove, and every unfamiliar ship on the horizon could be either friend or foe. The allure of the unknown was a siren call that no pirate could resist, driving them to venture beyond familiar shores and dive deep into the heart of the ocean.

In the realm of business, this allure of the unknown is equally compelling. The world of commerce is vast and ever-changing, with new markets emerging, consumer preferences evolving, and technological advancements reshaping industries. For entrepreneurs and business leaders, the unknown represents untapped potential, unexplored opportunities, and the chance to innovate and redefine the status quo.

Real World Business Examples of "The Allure of the Unknown: Venturing Beyond Safe Harbors":

SpaceX and the Commercial Space Industry: Elon Musk founded SpaceX with the aim of making space travel more affordable and, eventually, colonizing Mars. Despite initial setbacks, the allure of exploring the unknown boundaries of space pushed Musk and his team to innovate. SpaceX has since achieved significant milestones, such as the successful

- landing and reuse of its Falcon rockets and sending astronauts to the International Space Station.

- Apple and the iPhone: In the early 2000s, the mobile phone market was dominated by companies like Nokia and BlackBerry. Apple, primarily known for its computers and iPods, ventured into the unknown territory of smartphones. Despite skepticism, the iPhone was unveiled in 2007 and

Figure 2- Midjourney(2023)

- revolutionized the industry with its touch interface and app ecosystem. (Apple, 2007)

- Amazon and E-commerce: In its early days, Amazon was a simple online bookstore. The idea of buying books online was unfamiliar to many consumers. Yet, the allure of the vast untapped potential of online retail pushed Jeff Bezos to expand Amazon's offerings. Today, Amazon stands as a testament to venturing beyond known territories, encompassing everything from e-commerce to cloud computing. (DePillis & Sherman, 2018)

Historical Pirate Examples of "The Allure of the Unknown: Venturing Beyond Safe Harbors":

- Blackbeard (Edward Teach): Perhaps one of the most notorious pirates, Blackbeard roamed the Atlantic and Caribbean. His reputation for ruthlessness and the legends of his buried treasures drew many to the life of piracy. His adventurous spirit and appetite for the unknown is evident in his audacious exploits, like blockading the port of Charleston.

- Captain Kidd: Originally a privateer, Captain William Kidd became infamous for his alleged turn to piracy. He sailed to various parts of the world, from the Caribbean to the Indian Ocean. The lure of the unknown was evident when he ventured to the waters around Madagascar, an area replete with legends of pirate treasures. (NY Times, 2000)

- Anne Bonny and Mary Read: These two female pirates defied the conventions of their time. Not only were they among the few women in piracy, but they also ventured into a world unknown to most women of their era. Their partnership, bravery, and skill in battle made them legendary figures. Their choice to pursue a life of piracy, with all its perils and promises, epitomizes the allure of the unknown. (Simon, 2022)

Both in piracy and business, venturing beyond familiar territories often comes with its set of challenges and risks. But as history has shown, it is often those who are brave enough to face the unknown that end up shaping the future.

2. Embracing Risks: The Intricate Dance of Danger and Opportunity

The life of a pirate was a symphony of unpredictability, where each day brought with it new challenges and uncertainties. The vast expanse of the ocean was both their playground and battlefield, where every decision could lead to unparalleled treasures or unforeseen perils. The allure of uncharted territories, the promise of untold riches, and the ever-present shadow of danger made their journeys a testament to the human spirit's audacity. Every raid was a calculated risk, every storm faced a test of their mettle, and every treasure discovered a reward for their bravery.

Similarly, the realm of business is not for the faint-hearted. It demands a pioneering spirit, akin to that of the pirates, where entrepreneurs must navigate the turbulent waters of market dynamics, competition, and innovation. Just as pirates weighed the risks of their voyages against the potential bounty, entrepreneurs must assess the viability of their ventures against potential setbacks. The thrill lies not just in the destination but in the journey itself - the challenges faced, the obstacles overcome, and the innovations pioneered.

Yet, it's essential to understand that both pirates and entrepreneurs don't embrace risks recklessly. Behind every daring raid or business venture lies meticulous planning, strategy, and an innate understanding of the environment. The high stakes in both worlds make the rewards sweeter, but they also underscore the importance of preparation, adaptability, and resilience. Whether it's the promise of buried treasure or market success, the journey is a dance of danger and opportunity, where the brave not only survive but thrive.

Real World Business Examples of "Embracing Risks: The Intricate Dance of Danger and Opportunity ":

- Netflix's Transition to Streaming: In its early days, Netflix was a mail-order DVD service. However, seeing the potential of the internet, CEO Reed Hastings took the considerable risk of pivoting towards streaming content online. This move, fraught with uncertainty given the dominant physical DVD market, eventually paid off, transforming the way we consume media and turning Netflix into an entertainment behemoth. (MISRA, 2020)

- Uber Breaking Traditional Transportation Norms: Travis Kalanick and Garrett Camp took a significant risk when they founded Uber. They challenged established transportation norms, often operating in legal gray areas or even in direct violation of local regulations. This bold risk-taking approach led to numerous legal battles and controversies. However, the potential reward of redefining urban transportation worldwide has turned Uber into a multi-billion-dollar entity. (Blystone, 2023)

- Airbnb and the Concept of Home Sharing: Brian Chesky, Nathan Blecharczyk, and Joe Gebbia took a leap of faith when they started Airbnb. They banked on the idea that people would be willing to open their homes to strangers. The risks were evident: concerns about safety, potential property damages, and legal battles with hotel associations and city regulators. Despite these challenges, Airbnb's gamble led to a revolutionary shift in the hospitality industry. (LEWIS, 2021)

Historical Pirate Examples of "Embracing Risks: The Intricate Dance of Danger and Opportunity ":

- Sir Francis Drake: Before he was knighted, Drake was seen by many as a pirate due to his frequent raids on Spanish ships and settlements. He took significant risks, most notably his circumnavigation of the globe between 1577 and 1580. This journey was fraught with dangers, from confrontations with the Spanish to the unpredictable nature of uncharted waters. However, the rewards, both in terms of plunder and the acclaim he received upon his return to England, were monumental. (Fernandez-Armesto, n.d.)

- Bartholomew Roberts ("Black Bart"): In a short but intense period of piracy, Roberts captured over 400 ships. He was known for his audacity, often attacking heavily fortified merchant ships and towns. While the risks of such confrontations were high, the potential rewards in terms of plunder made his aggressive approach worthwhile. (thewayofthepirates.com, n.d.)

- Calico Jack Rackham: Known for his distinctive flag featuring a skull with crossed swords, Calico Jack was also known for his daring escapades. One of his most audacious acts was the theft of an anchored sloop right from under the noses of its crew. While such daring ventures elevated his status among pirates, they also increased the risks of capture. (history.co.uk, n.d.)

Both in the worlds of piracy and business, individuals have demonstrated that with high risks come high rewards. Those willing to face danger and uncertainty head-on, whether in search of treasure or entrepreneurial success, often find themselves at the forefront of change and innovation.

3. The Spirit of Freedom: Navigating the Waters of Autonomy and Legacy

The boundless expanse of the oceans was more than just a physical space for pirates; it was a symbol of unbridled freedom and endless possibilities. Far from the shackles of societal norms and the rigid structures of the mainland, the seas offered an escape, a realm where one's destiny was not dictated by birthright or class but by courage and cunning. Pirates reveled in this autonomy, crafting their own narratives, setting their own moral compasses, and living by codes they deemed fit. This wasn't just about rebellion; it was about reclaiming agency, about asserting one's right to determine their own fate amidst the vastness of the sea.

Similarly, the world of business, especially for entrepreneurs, is a vast ocean of opportunities, fraught with challenges but also brimming with potential. Entrepreneurs, akin to the pirates of yore, are not content with following pre-charted maps or adhering to established blueprints. They are visionaries, driven by a burning desire to carve out their own niche, to disrupt the status quo, and to innovate in spaces others might overlook. The entrepreneurial journey is not just about financial gains or market shares; it's about the freedom to dream, to create, and to shape the future on one's own terms.

- **Challenging the Horizon:** Just as pirates ventured into the unknown, braving uncharted territories and mysterious islands, entrepreneurs push the boundaries of innovation, often stepping into industries or niches that many might deem too risky or unconventional.

- **Re-writing the Script:** Pirates defied societal norms and the established order. In the same vein, entrepreneurs often challenge existing business practices, bringing fresh perspectives and rewriting the industry's script with groundbreaking ideas.

- **Crafting a Legacy:** Beyond the lure of treasure and adventure, many pirates sought to leave a legacy, to be remembered through tales and legends. Entrepreneurs are similarly driven, not just by monetary success but by the urge to create something lasting, to leave an impact that transcends their own tenure.

- **Collaborative Freedom:** While pirates formed crews and alliances to achieve common goals, entrepreneurs understand the importance of collaboration. True freedom in business doesn't mean going it alone; it means building strong teams, fostering partnerships, and creating synergies that allow for collective growth.

- **Guided by a Vision:** Pirates, though often portrayed as whimsical, were guided by clear goals, whether seeking a fabled treasure or a particular territory. Entrepreneurs, too, must have a clear vision, a beacon that guides them through tumultuous waters and keeps them anchored amidst the storms.

- **Embracing the Dual Role:** Much like a pirate captain who had to inspire the crew and also ensure discipline, entrepreneurs walk the tightrope of being visionaries and pragmatists. They are dreamers who see potential where others see challenges, but they are also grounded realists, keenly aware of market dynamics, risks, and the importance of adaptability.

In essence, the spirit of freedom in the entrepreneurial realm, much like the pirates' love for the sea, is a blend of passion, autonomy, and responsibility. It's about carving out one's own path while being cognizant of the broader implications, ensuring that the journey is not just successful but also meaningful.

Yet, it's crucial to recognize that with this freedom comes responsibility. Just as pirates had to navigate treacherous waters, face formidable foes, and make ethical choices, entrepreneurs too must grapple with the challenges of their chosen path. They must make decisions that balance their vision with the needs of their stakeholders, the environment, and the broader community. But in this intricate dance between freedom and responsibility, between risk and reward, lies the true essence of the entrepreneurial spirit: the relentless pursuit of one's own vision, fueled by passion, resilience, and a desire to leave an indelible mark on the world.

Figure 3- Midjourney(2023)

Real World Business Examples of "The Spirit of Freedom: Navigating the Waters of Autonomy and Legacy ":

- Richard Branson and the Virgin Group: Richard Branson's entrepreneurial journey embodies the spirit of freedom. From starting a student magazine to building the Virgin brand, which spans multiple industries from music to airlines to space travel, Branson has consistently demonstrated a desire to break free from conventions, take risks, and chart his own course.

- Ritesh Agarwal and OYO Rooms: At a young age, Ritesh Agarwal founded OYO Rooms, a platform to standardize and brand budget hotels in India. Going against established hotel chains and industry norms, he embraced the spirit of freedom to disrupt the hospitality industry, growing OYO into a global brand. (Soni, 2015)

- Sara Blakely and Spanx: Starting with an idea to improve undergarments for women, Sara Blakely invested her savings to create Spanx. Instead of following traditional routes in the fashion industry, she charted her own course, eventually building a billion-dollar brand and redefining shapewear for women. (MasterClass, 2022)

Historical Pirate Examples of "The Spirit of Freedom: Navigating the Waters of Autonomy and Legacy ":

- Captain Henry Avery: In the late 17th century, Avery led a mutiny against his oppressive officers and took command of the ship. Embracing the spirit of freedom, he embarked on a piracy spree, most notably capturing the Grand Mughal ship Ganj-i-Sawai, which was laden with immense wealth. Avery's desire to chart his own destiny made him one of the wealthiest pirates of his time, though his ultimate fate remains a mystery. (Cartwright, 2021)

- Jean Lafitte: A pirate and privateer in the Gulf of Mexico, Lafitte was known for establishing his own pirate colony called Barataria Bay. Rejecting traditional societal constraints, he created a haven for pirates, smugglers, and those who sought freedom from the established order. His autonomous rule and defense of New Orleans during the War of 1812 further solidified his legend. (National Parks Service, 2020)

- Ching Shih: One of the most powerful pirates in history, Ching Shih commanded a fleet of hundreds of ships with tens of thousands of pirates under her rule. She started as a commoner but rose to power by asserting her authority, establishing a strict code of conduct for her fleet, and successfully negotiating with the Chinese government. Her leadership epitomized the spirit of charting one's own course. (Banerji, 2022)

In both the pirate and business worlds, the drive to break free from societal norms, to challenge the status quo, and to carve out a unique path showcases the timeless human desire for freedom and autonomy. Whether on the open seas or in the boardroom, this spirit continues to inspire and drive individuals towards greatness.

As we drop anchor and reflect upon the tales and lessons of this chapter, it becomes evident that the spirit of adventure, risk-taking, and freedom is not just the domain of pirates but is deeply ingrained in the DNA of successful entrepreneurs and business leaders. The high seas, with their unpredictable challenges and boundless horizons, mirror the business landscape of today. Just as pirates navigated through treacherous waters, faced formidable foes, and sought hidden treasures, modern businesses too face a myriad of challenges, competitors, and opportunities. The tales of pirates, filled with audacity, cunning, and an unyielding spirit, serve as a beacon, illuminating the path for those who dare to venture into the world of business.

The parallels between the world of piracy and the realm of business are striking. Both demand a certain level of audacity, a willingness to embrace risks, and the vision to see opportunities where others see challenges. Pirates, with their insatiable thirst for adventure and their relentless pursuit of freedom, epitomize the essence of what it takes to succeed in any endeavor. Their tales, filled with daring exploits, cunning strategies, and an undying spirit, serve as a testament to the power of determination, adaptability, and vision. In the world of business, these very qualities set apart the visionaries from the rest, the trailblazers from the followers, and the legends from the ordinary.

Captain Martin Marlinspike, with his wealth of experiences and his unique perspective, often emphasizes the importance of embracing the pirate's spirit in the world of business. "In the vast ocean of commerce, as on the high seas,"he muses, "it's not the size of the ship that determines success, but the spirit of the sailor." As you chart your course in the world of business, may you embrace this spirit, allowing it to guide you, inspire you, and propel you towards uncharted horizons filled with promise, potential, and unparalleled success. Until our paths cross again in the next chapter, may your sails be ever full, your compass ever true, and may fortune favor the bold!

Chapter 2: "The Code is More What You'd Call 'Guidelines' Than Actual Rules" - The Flexibility and Adaptability in Business

Yo Ho Yo Ho! once again, esteemed readers! As we continue our voyage through the intricate tapestry of business, guided by the age-old wisdom of pirates, we find ourselves exploring the realm of flexibility and adaptability. The world of piracy, with its tales of audacious raids, cunning strategies, and legendary treasures, has always captivated the imagination. But beneath the surface of these tales lies a deeper truth. Pirates, for all their notoriety, were masters of adaptability. They thrived in an ever-changing environment, constantly evolving their strategies, tactics, and even their very codes of conduct. This fluidity, this ability to adapt and pivot, is a lesson that finds profound relevance in today's dynamic business landscape.

In the unpredictable waters of the Caribbean and beyond, pirates often found themselves facing unforeseen challenges. From treacherous storms to unexpected encounters with rival pirates or naval fleets, the seas were a theater of constant change. Yet, these pirates, with their iconic Jolly Roger flags and fearsome reputations, were not just survivors but thrivers. They understood that rigidity was a luxury they couldn't afford. Their codes, often romanticized in tales and legends, were not set in stone. They were guidelines, flexible frameworks that allowed them to navigate the complexities of their world. This inherent flexibility, this understanding that change was the only constant, was a cornerstone of their success. And it's this very principle that modern businesses must embrace. In a world marked by rapid technological advancements, shifting consumer preferences, and global challenges, the ability to adapt, to be flexible, and to pivot when necessary is not just an asset; it's a necessity.

Now, you might wonder, how can the codes of pirates, with their fluidity and adaptability, be applied to the structured world of business? The parallels are more profound than one might initially perceive. Just as pirates had to be nimble, adjusting their sails to the changing winds, businesses today must be agile, ready to adapt to the ever-evolving market dynamics. The most successful enterprises are those that don't just react to change but anticipate it, embrace it, and harness it to their advantage. They understand that in the world of business, much like on the high seas, rigidity can be a downfall. Flexibility, on the other hand, can open doors to new opportunities, new markets, and new horizons.

So, as we delve deeper into this chapter, let's draw inspiration from the pirates of old. Let's learn from their ability to adapt, their willingness to change, and their understanding of the importance of flexibility. For in the world of business, as in the world of piracy, it's those who can ride the waves of change, who can adjust their sails to the shifting winds, and who can navigate the unpredictable currents, that truly leave a lasting legacy. Join me, dear reader, on this enlightening journey, as we explore the importance of flexibility and adaptability in business, guided by the timeless wisdom of pirates.

1. The Essence of Adaptability: Steering Through Unfamiliar Tides

The vast oceans, with their ever-changing moods and mysteries, often presented pirates with scenarios that no map had prepared them for. Uncharted islands, unpredictable storms, and unforeseen adversaries were all part of a pirate's journey. In such situations, a rigid adherence to plans could spell disaster. Pirates, with their survival instincts honed to perfection, understood the significance of adaptability, of recalibrating their strategies based on the challenges at hand, and of making swift decisions that prioritized the safety and success of their crew.

Drawing parallels to the business world, leaders today often find themselves navigating through similarly uncharted territories. Emerging technologies, shifting consumer preferences, and evolving market dynamics can turn established strategies on their heads. In such volatile environments, adaptability becomes a leader's most potent weapon, allowing them to pivot, innovate, and steer their organizations towards success even when the traditional playbook falls short.

Real World Business Examples of "The Essence of Adaptability: Steering Through Unfamiliar Tides":

- Nokia's Transition from Paper to Telecommunications: Nokia began as a pulp mill in the 19th century, transitioning through several industries like rubber and cable before becoming a telecommunications giant. While it faced challenges in the smartphone era, Nokia's history is a testament to adaptability and the ability to steer through multiple industry changes successfully. (Finley, 2016)

- Adobe's Shift to Subscription Models: Adobe Systems, known for its software products like Photoshop and Acrobat, made a significant pivot by transitioning from selling software licenses to a cloud-based subscription model with Adobe Creative Cloud. This move, in response to the changing dynamics of the software industry, not only increased its revenue but also enhanced its customer relations by offering regular updates and added services. (Moorman, 2018)

- Microsoft's Evolution Under Satya Nadella: When Satya Nadella took over as CEO of Microsoft, the tech giant was struggling to maintain its relevance in a rapidly changing industry. Nadella steered Microsoft towards cloud computing, focusing on products like Azure and Office 365. His leadership and adaptability transformed the company's trajectory, making it a dominant force in cloud services. (Tabrizi, 2023)

Historical Pirate Examples of "The Essence of Adaptability: Steering Through Unfamiliar Tides":

- Black Bart (Bartholomew Roberts): Bartholomew Roberts, often considered one of the most successful pirates, showed incredible adaptability during his career. When faced with formidable naval ships, he often changed tactics, opting for stealth and cunning over direct confrontation. His ability to adapt his strategies based on the situation allowed him to capture over 400 ships during his tenure as a pirate. (Cartwright, 2021)

- Samuel Bellamy and the Whydah: Samuel Bellamy, known for his brief yet prolific pirate career, was notable for his use of the Whydah Gally, a former slave ship. Recognizing the ship's potential, he repurposed it into a formidable pirate ship. His ability to see beyond a ship's original purpose and adapt it to his needs showcased his adaptability. (Wikipedia, n.d.)

- Anne Dieu-le-Veut: Known as the "Caribbean Amazon," Anne was a pirate in the late 17th century who showcased her adaptability by switching allegiances and tactics as needed. Initially a criminal deported to the Caribbean, she shifted to piracy after her husband's death. Her ability to adapt and survive in the male-dominated world of piracy made her a legend. (Wikipedia, n.d.)

Whether navigating the unpredictable seas or steering a business through changing landscapes, adaptability remains a vital skill. It allows individuals and organizations to evolve, overcome challenges, and find success even when faced with unfamiliar situations.

2. Navigating Ambiguities: The Delicate Balance of Flexibility and Integrity

The world of piracy, often romanticized in tales of high-seas adventures, was more nuanced than the black-and-white narratives suggest. While pirates did operate outside the laws of nations, they weren't anarchists without any guiding principles. They had their own codes, a unique set of ethics that governed their interactions and decisions. Yet, these codes were malleable, designed to be interpreted rather than rigidly followed. This inherent flexibility was a strength, allowing pirates to adapt to the ever-changing dynamics of the sea, to make choices that prioritized the collective good of the crew, and to find innovative solutions to challenges that didn't fit traditional molds.

Similarly, in the intricate tapestry of the corporate world, rigidity can often be a hindrance. Businesses operate in dynamic environments, facing challenges that can't always be addressed by standard operating procedures or traditional methodologies. Leaders, akin to pirate captains, must be adept at interpreting situations, understanding the nuances, and making decisions that might sometimes defy conventional wisdom. This doesn't mean compromising on integrity or values; rather, it's about understanding that real-world challenges often exist in shades of gray, requiring a blend of creativity, pragmatism, and ethical discernment.

However, with this flexibility comes a significant responsibility. Just as pirates had to ensure their interpretations didn't jeopardize the crew's trust or cohesion, business leaders must ensure that their decisions, even when navigating ambiguities, align with the organization's ethos and stakeholder expectations. It's a delicate dance, one that demands a keen sense of judgment, a commitment to the organization's core principles, and the courage to venture into uncharted waters when the situation demands.

Real World Business Examples of "Flexibility in Interpretation: The Delicate Balance of Flexibility and Integrity ":

- Apple's iPhone App Store Guidelines: Apple's App Store guidelines are comprehensive, but they often leave room for interpretation. Over the years, Apple has been flexible in its enforcement, sometimes allowing apps that technically violate the guidelines but offer unique or beneficial features. This discretion allows Apple to maintain a diverse ecosystem while adhering to its core values.

- Google's Approach to "Don't Be Evil": Google's famous guiding principle has been open to interpretation over the years. While it provides a broad moral compass, the company has, at times, made decisions that toe the line of this mantra, such as its ventures into China. By interpreting this principle flexibly, Google aims to maximize its reach while staying true to its foundational ethos. (Zubrow, 2023)

- Tesla's Direct-to-Consumer Sales Model: In many places, it's customary (or even legally required) for automakers to sell vehicles through dealerships. Tesla, however, opted for a direct-to-consumer model, navigating the gray areas of legislation in various states and countries. This approach, while controversial, allows Tesla to control the customer experience and pricing more effectively. (Neiger, 2022)

Historical Pirate Examples of "Flexibility in Interpretation: The Delicate Balance of Flexibility and Integrity ":

- Pirate Codes: While pirates like Bartholomew Roberts had their own set of codes, these were more guidelines than strict rules. For instance, while the code might dictate the distribution of spoils, there were always exceptions based on the situation, injuries sustained, or the value of the capture. This flexibility ensured fairness and kept the crew united. (Wikipedia, n.d.)

- Captain Kidd's Privateering License: Captain William Kidd began his maritime career as a privateer, possessing a license from the English crown to attack enemy ships. However, the line between privateering and piracy was thin, and his ability to interpret his license flexibly was both an asset and, ultimately, a liability. (Cartwright, 2021)

- The Republic of Pirates in Nassau: In the early 18th century, Nassau became a haven for pirates, essentially operating as its independent entity. While they had their own set of rules and governance, the pirates of Nassau were known to interpret treaties and agreements with European powers flexibly, often to their advantage. (piratesofnassau.com, n.d.)

Figure 4- Midjourney(2023)

Whether on the high seas or in the boardroom, the ability to interpret rules flexibly and navigate gray areas is essential. It allows for adaptability and ensures that decisions can be made in the best interest of the collective, even when faced with ambiguity.

3. Innovation as the Beacon of Adaptability

In the world of piracy, innovation was more than just a buzzword; it was a way of life. Pirates, always on the lookout for an edge over their adversaries, constantly sought innovative solutions to the challenges they faced. Whether it was devising new tactics for battle, crafting ingenious tools to aid in navigation, or finding novel ways to communicate across ships, innovation was at the heart of a pirate's existence.

In the realm of business, the spirit of innovation is what sets industry leaders apart from the rest. In a world that's constantly evolving, companies that foster a culture of innovation, that encourage out-of-the-box thinking, and that are open to change are the ones that thrive and lead their industries.

Real World Business Examples of "Innovation as the Beacon of Adaptability":

- Amazon's Transition from Books to E-commerce Giant: Starting as an online bookstore, Amazon's relentless pursuit of innovation transformed it into the world's most prominent e-commerce platform. From introducing the Kindle to revolutionizing logistics with Prime and venturing into cloud computing with AWS, Amazon's adaptability is rooted in its innovative spirit. (capitalism.com, 2022)

- Netflix's Shift from DVD Rentals to Streaming: Originally a mail-order DVD rental service, Netflix's foresight and innovation led it to pioneer online streaming, completely transforming the entertainment industry. Their continued innovation, including producing original content, has kept them at the forefront of the industry. (Chadwick, 2023)

- SpaceX's Reusable Rockets: While the concept of space travel isn't new, SpaceX, under Elon Musk's leadership, innovated by developing reusable rocket technology. This dramatically reduces the cost of space missions and represents a significant leap in the commercial space industry.

Historical Pirate Examples of "Innovation as the Beacon of Adaptability":

- Blackbeard's Use of Fear Tactics: Edward Teach, known as Blackbeard, used innovation in psychological warfare. He would light slow-burning fuses in his beard, creating a smoky, demonic appearance during battle. This innovative tactic intimidated his enemies, often giving him an advantage without needing to resort to physical violence.

- Pirate Ship Design and Modifications: Pirates often modified captured ships to suit their specific needs. They would increase speed by reducing weight, add more cannons for firepower, and make structural changes to improve maneuverability. This constant innovation gave pirate ships a distinct edge during naval confrontations. (Minster, 2019)

- Pirate Signals and Communication: Pirates developed unique signals to communicate across ships, using combinations of flags and lanterns. This innovative form of communication allowed them to coordinate attacks, share information about potential targets, or warn fellow pirates about imminent threats. (marshadelamothe, 2023)

In both the pirate and business worlds, innovation is not just about introducing new products or services. It's about rethinking how things are done, finding better solutions to existing problems, and anticipating future challenges. Those who embrace and champion innovation are often the ones who stay ahead of the curve and define the direction of their respective domains.

4. Bending, Not Breaking: The Art of Interpretation

Pirates, while often seen as lawless, did have their own codes. However, these codes were not rigid. They were seen more as guidelines, open to interpretation based on the situation at hand. This flexibility allowed pirates to make decisions that were in the best interest of their crew and their mission.

In business, while rules and protocols are essential, there's also value in interpretation. Leaders must know when to stick to the rulebook and when to think outside the box, ensuring the company's best interests are always at the forefront.

- **The Spirit of the Law:** Just as pirates often interpreted their codes to fit the situation, business leaders should understand the spirit behind rules and regulations. It's about grasping the fundamental essence or intention behind a rule rather than sticking to its literal interpretation. By doing this, decisions can be made that respect the rule's intent while allowing for creative solutions.

- **Situational Flexibility:** The business landscape is ever-evolving, and unforeseen challenges arise regularly. In such scenarios, a rigid adherence to protocols can be a hindrance. Leaders need to be adaptable, assessing each situation on its merits and being willing to bend the rules if it means achieving the best outcome for the organization.

- **Balancing Act:** The art of interpretation is essentially a balancing act between consistency and flexibility. While consistency provides stability and predictability, flexibility allows for innovation and rapid response to changing circumstances.

- **Guided Discretion:** While discretion in interpretation is valuable, it should be guided. Parameters can be set to ensure that while there's room for flexibility, there's no compromise on the company's core values or legal obligations.

- **Learning from the Outcomes**: Every interpretation and subsequent decision leads to an outcome. It's essential for businesses to analyze these outcomes, understanding what went right or wrong, and use these insights for future decision-making processes.

- **Feedback Loops:** Encouraging feedback from different levels of the organization can provide a holistic view of how certain rules impact operations. This can lead to better interpretation guidelines and even changes to rules that might be outdated or redundant.

- **Risk and Reward:** The flexibility of interpretation does come with its risks. However, calculated risks often lead to innovation and growth. By evaluating the potential rewards against the risks, leaders can make informed decisions about when to bend and when to stand firm.

Real World Business Examples of "Bending, Not Breaking: The Art of Interpretation":

- Airbnb's Regulatory Battles: As Airbnb grew, it found itself in regulatory gray areas in many cities where short-term rentals were not clearly defined by local laws. Instead of completely withdrawing, Airbnb often engaged with these cities, interpreting and bending its business model to fit local requirements, and sometimes even helping shape new regulations. (O'Sullivan & Loudis, 2023)

- Uber's Entry into Global Markets: Uber, when entering various international markets, faced numerous regulatory hurdles.

Traditional taxi services and local laws often posed challenges. Rather than adhering strictly to their established model, Uber adapted its services to fit different markets—introducing auto-rickshaws in India or boat services in cities with waterways, for example. (Manangi, 2017)

- Pharmaceutical "Off-Label" Uses: In the pharmaceutical industry, drugs approved for one condition are sometimes discovered to have benefits for other conditions. While marketing a drug for non-approved uses is illegal, doctors can prescribe it "off-label." Companies, while careful not to promote off-label uses directly, will often fund research, and ensure information is available for these alternative uses, bending the traditional boundaries of drug marketing. (Miller, 2009)

Historical Pirate Examples of "Bending, Not Breaking: The Art of Interpretation":

- Pirate Pardons: In various periods, governments offered pirates pardons to curb piracy. Some pirates like Calico Jack took advantage of these offers temporarily, bending their pirate codes to accept royal pardons, only to return to piracy when the conditions suited them.

- Pirate Havens and Collaborations: While pirates were outlaws on the high seas, many ports turned a blind eye to their activities, offering them refuge. Places like Port Royal became notorious pirate havens. Pirates and local governments often entered unspoken agreements; pirates provided goods and wealth influx, and in return, local authorities would interpret laws flexibly, allowing pirates to operate without much interference.

- "No Prey, No Pay" Rule: The traditional pirate code dictated that the crew received shares of the captured loot. However, in times when captures were scarce, pirate captains often had to bend this rule, ensuring that their crew was taken care of, sometimes even from their pockets or through other ventures.

In the end, the art of interpretation in business, much like in piracy, is about navigating the gray areas. It's about understanding that while rules and guidelines provide a necessary structure, true leadership often lies in the nuanced spaces between the lines, where decisions can mean the difference between stagnation and progress.

As we drop anchor on this chapter, the echoes of pirate wisdom reverberate, reminding us of the timeless value of adaptability and innovation. The high seas, with their unpredictable tides and treacherous storms, were a testament to the ever-changing nature of life. Pirates, those audacious navigators of these waters, understood that to survive and thrive, one had to be flexible, willing to change course when needed, and always ready to innovate. Their tales, filled with daring exploits and cunning strategies, serve as a beacon for modern leaders, illuminating the path to success in today's dynamic business landscape.

In the vast ocean of business, much like in the world of piracy, it's not always the strongest or the most resourceful that succeed; it's those who can adapt, who can ride the winds of change, and who can turn challenges into opportunities. Companies and leaders that embody this spirit of adaptability, that view rules as guidelines and that prioritize innovation, are the ones that stand the test of time. They not only navigate the challenges of the present but also set the course for the future, charting new horizons, and exploring uncharted territories.

Captain Martin Marlinspike, with his wealth of experiences from both the world of piracy and the corporate realm, often emphasizes the importance of being fluid, of being like water, which takes the shape of its container but also has the power to carve mountains. As you continue your corporate voyage, may you imbibe this wisdom, allowing adaptability and innovation to be your guiding stars. May you have the courage to venture into uncharted waters, the wisdom to know when to change course, and the vision to see opportunities where others see challenges.

Until our paths cross again in another chapter of this enlightening journey, may your sails always catch the wind, may your compass always point true, and may success be your constant companion on this grand adventure called business. Fair winds and following seas, dear reader!

Chapter 3: "Honor Among Thieves" - The Importance of Trust and Integrity in Business

Ahoy, my esteemed colleagues of the corporate realm! Captain Martin Marlinspike here, extending a warm invitation to yet another chapter of our ongoing voyage. As we've journeyed together through the annals of pirate wisdom, we've unearthed many a gem that shines brightly in the world of business. Today, we set our sights on a principle that might seem at odds with the very essence of piracy, yet is deeply ingrained in the fabric of their world: "Honor Among Thieves." This age-old adage, whispered amidst the creaking of ship timbers and the rustling of treasure maps, speaks of a code, an unspoken bond that even the fiercest pirates adhered to.

Now, one might wonder, how can there be honor among those who live by the sword, who plunder without remorse? But delve deeper, and you'll find that even in the treacherous world of piracy, trust was the currency more valuable than gold. A pirate's reputation, their very standing among their peers, hinged on their ability to be trustworthy, to uphold their end of bargains, and to stand by their crew in the face of danger. It was this trust, this bond of honor, that often determined their success or doom on the high seas.

Drawing parallels to the modern business landscape, the echoes of this principle are unmistakable. In the intricate dance of corporate dealings, amidst mergers, acquisitions, and partnerships, trust remains the cornerstone. It's the silent contract that seals deals, the invisible thread that binds partnerships, and the foundation upon which empires are built. As we delve into this chapter, we'll explore the nuances of this trust, understanding its importance, its implications, and its undeniable value in the world of business. So, with the wind in our sails and the horizon beckoning, let's embark on this journey, with me, Captain Martin Marlinspike, as your trusted guide.

1. Building Trust: The Foundation of All Relationships

In the heart of every pirate, from the seasoned captains to the greenest deckhands, lay a burning desire for treasure. But beyond this tangible wealth, there was another form of treasure, intangible yet invaluable: trust. Pirates operated in a world of uncertainty, where danger lurked at every corner and alliances were as shifting as the sands. In such a world, a captain's word became the anchor, the one constant that the crew could rely on. When a captain made a promise to his crew, be it a share of the loot or a course of action, it was expected to be honored. This trust between captain and crew was the glue that held them together, ensuring loyalty even in the face of danger.

Similarly, in the corporate world, the landscape might be different, but the principle remains the same. Trust is the foundation upon which relationships, be it with clients, partners, or employees, are built. In boardrooms and business meetings, a leader's word, much like a pirate captain's, becomes their bond. When leaders make commitments, stakeholders expect them to be honored. This mutual trust is what drives collaborations, seals deals, and fosters long-term partnerships.

Real World Business Examples of "Building Trust: The Foundation of All Relationships":

- Warren Buffet and Handshake Deals: Warren Buffet, the chairman of Berkshire Hathaway, is known for closing multi-billion-dollar deals based on trust and handshakes. His simple and straightforward approach to business, paired with his history of integrity, has made him a trusted figure in the corporate world. Stakeholders and partners know that if Buffet gives his word, it's as good as gold. (Hargreaves, 2019)

- Johnson & Johnson's Tylenol Crisis: In 1982, when seven people died after consuming cyanide-laced Tylenol capsules, Johnson & Johnson swiftly took action. The company recalled 31 million bottles of Tylenol and introduced tamper-proof packaging. Their immediate and transparent response, prioritizing consumer safety over immediate profits, helped maintain and even strengthen the public's trust in the brand. (Knight, 1982)

- Zappos and Customer Service: Zappos, an online shoe retailer, has built its brand around unparalleled customer service. They offer a 365-day return policy, free shipping, and emphasize the importance of forming genuine connections with customers. By going above and beyond for their customers consistently, they've cultivated immense trust and loyalty. (Frampton, 2020)

Historical Pirate Examples of "Building Trust: The Foundation of All Relationships":

- Black Bart's Code of Conduct: Bartholomew Roberts, also known as Black Bart, was one of the most successful pirates. He had a set of pirate codes that ensured fair distribution of loot, rules for behavior onboard, and a framework for resolving disputes. This code helped establish trust among his crew, which was critical for their collective success.

37

- Captain Kidd and Mutinous Crew: Captain William Kidd's initial voyage as a privateer turned rocky when he failed to capture valuable prizes. His crew grew mutinous, so in an effort to regain their trust, Kidd captured an Armenian ship. Though this capture led to accusations of piracy, it showcased the lengths a captain might go to maintain his crew's trust.

- Mary Read and Anne Bonny: In a male-dominated world of piracy, Mary Read and Anne Bonny forged a bond built on trust. Disguised as men, they sailed together under Calico Jack. Their mutual trust was evident when they stood side by side in battles, even when the rest of the crew retreated.

Trust, whether among pirates or in boardrooms, serves as the bedrock of relationships and is integral to the successful navigation of challenges and the forging of lasting bonds.

2. Integrity in Actions: Walking the Talk

Promises and proclamations are but words, and in the world of piracy, words alone held little weight. It was actions that spoke volumes. A pirate captain could promise the world, but if his actions didn't align with his words, he'd quickly lose the trust and respect of his crew. This emphasis on actions over words was a cornerstone of pirate culture. It ensured accountability, fostered trust, and built reputations. Pirates knew that to truly earn respect and trust, they had to walk the talk, ensuring that their deeds matched their promises.

In the realm of business, this principle of integrity in actions is paramount. Companies and leaders are constantly under scrutiny, with stakeholders watching their every move. In such an environment, it's not enough to make promises or set lofty goals.

Leaders and organizations must act with integrity, ensuring that their actions align with their words, values, and commitments.

Figure 5- Midjourney(2023)

Real World Business Examples of "Integrity in Actions: Walking the Talk":

- Patagonia's Environmental Commitment: Outdoor apparel brand Patagonia is well-known for its commitment to the environment. More than just marketing, they have consistently backed up their claims with actions, such as donating 1% of their annual sales to environmental causes, using sustainable materials, and openly advocating for environmental policies. (Wolfe, 2023)

- Starbucks and Ethical Sourcing: Starbucks has committed itself to ethical sourcing of its coffee beans. Their C.A.F.E. (Coffee and Farmer Equity) practices are designed to ensure that coffee farmers are treated fairly, and the environment is protected. Over the years, Starbucks has taken significant steps to ensure a large percentage of their coffee is ethically sourced and verified by third-party checks. (Starbucks, 2020)

- LEGO's Sustainable Initiatives: LEGO, the toy brick manufacturer, committed to making its products more sustainable. True to their word, the company has invested in developing sustainable materials for its bricks and aims to make its products from sustainable materials by 2030. (Wilson, 2021)

Historical Pirate Examples of "Integrity in Actions: Walking the Talk":

- Blackbeard's Blockade: Edward Teach, better known as Blackbeard, is infamous for his fearsome reputation. However, he was also known to keep his word. In 1718, Blackbeard blockaded the port of Charleston, South Carolina, and demanded medical supplies in exchange for hostages. As promised, once the supplies were delivered, he released the hostages unharmed.

- Samuel Bellamy and His Fairness: Known as "Black Sam" Bellamy, he was famed not just for his piracy but also for his democratic and fair treatment of his crew. Bellamy was known to prefer capturing ships without violence and treated prisoners fairly, often releasing them or giving them a choice to join his crew. His actions mirrored his beliefs in equality and justice.

- The Pirate Code: Pirates like Bartholomew Roberts and John Phillips had written codes of conduct for their crews. These were not mere words; they were followed strictly. Pirates knew that breaking the code could lead to punishments, ensuring that all members "walked the talk" when it came to abiding by the shared rules of the crew.

Both in the past and present, across different fields, the principle remains the same: integrity in actions is a hallmark of true leadership and is instrumental in building trust and respect.

3. The Long-Term Value of Trust and Integrity

For many pirates, the allure of the high seas wasn't just the promise of immediate riches; it was also the prospect of legends, of leaving behind a legacy that would be spoken of for generations. And in the world of piracy, legends weren't built on gold alone; they were built on trust and integrity. Pirates like Blackbeard or Calico Jack are remembered not just for their exploits, but for their characters, for the trust they inspired in their crews, and the codes they lived by. They understood that while treasures might provide immediate gratification, trust and integrity were the keys to lasting respect and legacy.

In the modern business landscape, this principle holds truer than ever. While quarterly profits and immediate gains are important, it's the long-term value of trust and integrity that truly sets companies apart. Brands that are trusted, that are known for their integrity, enjoy customer loyalty, positive word of mouth, and a reputation that can weather the toughest storms.

Real World Business Examples of "The Long-Term Value of Trust and Integrity":

- Johnson & Johnson's Tylenol Recall: In 1982, when seven people died after consuming cyanide-laced Tylenol capsules, Johnson & Johnson chose transparency and public safety over immediate profits. They recalled 31 million bottles of Tylenol, costing them over $100 million. This action strengthened the public's trust in the company, demonstrating that they prioritized consumer safety over profits. Years later, Tylenol remains a trusted brand, showcasing the long-term value of such trust and integrity. (NY Times, 2002)

- Costco's Employee Treatment: Costco is renowned for its treatment of employees, offering higher wages and benefits compared to many of its competitors in the retail sector. This dedication to ethical treatment has cultivated a loyal workforce with lower turnover rates, translating to a consistent shopping experience for customers. Over time, this has bolstered Costco's reputation and trustworthiness in the eyes of both its employees and customers. (Smedra, 2022)

- Apple's Stand on Privacy: Apple has consistently prioritized user privacy, even resisting pressure from government entities to unlock devices. Their commitment to user data privacy and security has fostered trust among its customer base, further solidifying its reputation as a company that values and protects its users' rights. (Leswing, 2021)

Historical Pirate Examples of "The Long-Term Value of Trust and Integrity":

- Bartholomew Roberts' Code of Conduct: Bartholomew Roberts, one of the most successful pirates of his time, had a strict code of conduct aboard his ship. This code not only regulated plunder and punishments but also prohibited activities like gambling, ensuring disputes and conflicts among the crew were minimized. His adherence to this code and fair treatment of his crew cemented his legacy as both a fearsome and just pirate.

- **Captain Kidd's Attempted Legitimacy:** Captain William Kidd began his maritime career as a privateer, working on behalf of the English crown. Even as accusations of piracy began to mount against him, Kidd was confident that he could clear his name by presenting the French passes he had acquired (proving that his captures were legal prizes). His trust in the system and his integrity in preserving these documents (despite them eventually failing to exonerate him) showed his commitment to his reputation and legacy.

- **Mary Read and Anne Bonny's Reputation:** Both Mary Read and Anne Bonny defied the gender norms of their time, earning respect and trust among their pirate peers not through deception but through their genuine skill, courage, and integrity. Their reputations were built not just on their piracy but on the trust they instilled among their crew and counterparts. Their stories are remembered for their courage and the integrity they showed in a male-dominated world.

Across eras and domains, the long-term value of trust and integrity has always been a cornerstone for those aiming to leave a lasting impact. Immediate gains may provide short-lived successes, but it's trust and integrity that lay the foundation for enduring legacies.

As our voyage through this chapter draws to a close, it's essential to cast our gaze back and reflect upon the treasures of wisdom we've unearthed. The world of piracy, with its tales of daring adventures and treacherous betrayals, offers a mirror to the corporate realm in more ways than one might initially perceive. At the heart of both these worlds lies a principle as old as time itself: the value of trust and integrity. While the high seas and boardrooms might seem worlds apart, the undercurrents of trust that flow through them bind them inextricably.

In the tales of pirates, where every new horizon brought with it unknown dangers and every ship on the horizon could be friend or foe, trust was the anchor that held crews together. It was the unspoken bond that ensured that a crew would stand by their captain, come hell or high water. It was the promise that agreements would be honored, that shares would be fair, and that every member of the crew, from the captain to the lowliest deckhand, would be treated with respect. This trust wasn't just a matter of principle; it was a matter of survival. For in the unpredictable world of piracy, where danger lurked at every corner, trust was the one constant that could be relied upon.

Drawing parallels to the corporate world, the echoes of this principle are profound. In a realm where competition is fierce, where companies vie for market share, and where every decision can have far-reaching implications, trust becomes the bedrock upon which empires are built. It's the silent promise that companies make to their stakeholders, the commitment that leaders give to their teams, and the bond that holds organizations together. In the long run, while strategies might change and markets might shift, it's trust and integrity that determine success. Companies that uphold these values, that walk the talk, and that prioritize long-term trust over short-term gains are the ones that stand the test of time.

In the words of Captain Martin Marlinspike, "Trust is the compass that guides us through the stormiest of seas, the anchor that holds us steady in the face of adversity." As we set sail towards new horizons and uncharted waters, may the lessons of trust and integrity be the guiding stars on your journey. For in the vast ocean of business, it's not just about reaching your destination; it's about the journey, the bonds you forge, and the legacy you leave behind. Until our next adventure, may your sails be ever full, and may your compass always point true!

Chapter 4: "No Prey, No Pay" - The Merits of Performance-Based Rewards in Business

Ahoy, my esteemed navigators of the intricate corporate waters! Our focus today is a principle that might sound simple but carries profound implications: "No Prey, No Pay." This age-old pirate code, echoing through the salty winds of history, encapsulates a truth that's as relevant on the high seas as it is in the high-rise offices of today's corporate giants.

In the golden age of piracy, when the Jolly Roger fluttered menacingly over the horizon, a pirate's fortune was never guaranteed. Their rewards were directly tied to their daring exploits, their cunning strategies, and, ultimately, their successes. If they returned to port empty-handed, there was no treasure to divide, no reward for their efforts. This direct correlation between effort and reward, risk, and return, is a concept deeply ingrained in today's performance-driven corporate culture. It's a world where bonuses, promotions, and accolades are often tied to tangible results, pushing individuals and teams to constantly strive for excellence.

However, as we set sail into this chapter, we'll delve deeper than just the surface implications of this mantra. We'll explore the nuances of performance-based rewards, the delicate balance leaders must strike to ensure fairness, and the broader impacts of such a system on organizational culture and individual motivation. So, tighten your grip on the wheel, brace yourself against the rolling waves of insight, and join me, Captain Martin Marlinspike, as we navigate the complex waters of "No Prey, No Pay" in the realm of business.

1. Motivation and Drive: The Heart of Performance-Based Rewards

In the heart of every pirate, from the seasoned captains to the greenest deckhands, lay a burning desire for treasure. This wasn't just about the glint of gold or the sparkle of jewels; it was about the promise of reward for their daring endeavors. The principle of "No Prey, No Pay" was a constant reminder that their fortunes were directly tied to their actions. If they strategized well, fought bravely, and outwitted their adversaries, they'd be rewarded handsomely. If not, they'd return to their hideouts with empty pockets and hungry bellies. This direct link between action and reward was a powerful motivator, pushing pirates to constantly hone their skills, collaborate effectively, and take calculated risks.

Similarly, in the corporate world, the promise of performance-based rewards serves as a potent motivator. Employees, much like pirates, are driven by the promise of rewards – be it monetary bonuses, promotions, or recognition. When they know that their efforts will be directly rewarded, they're more likely to push boundaries, innovate, and go the extra mile. It's a system that encourages proactivity, ambition, and a results-driven mindset.

Real World Business Examples of "Motivation and Drive: The Heart of Performance-Based Rewards":

- Sales Commissions: A classic example in the business world is the system of sales commissions. Salespeople are often offered a base salary, but the real allure lies in the commissions they can earn on top of this. The more they sell, the more they earn. This direct link between performance and reward drives salespeople to optimize their strategies, build better relationships, and push harder to close deals.

- Employee Stock Options: Many tech companies and startups offer employee stock options as part of their compensation packages. This gives employees a stake in the company's future. If the company does well and its valuation rises, the value of these stock options goes up, directly benefiting the employee. This setup encourages employees to invest their best efforts into the company, as its success directly translates to their personal financial success.

- Performance Bonuses: Across industries, companies set targets and goals for their teams. When these targets are met or exceeded, employees are rewarded with performance bonuses. These bonuses serve as an incentive for employees to consistently deliver high-quality work and achieve organizational objectives.

Historical Pirate Examples of "Motivation and Drive: The Heart of Performance-Based Rewards":

- Pirate Shares: Pirates operated on a system where the loot was divided based on shares. The captain and key officers would receive multiple shares due to their roles, while regular crew members received a single share. This system ensured that everyone had a stake in the success of the raid, and the promise of a larger share drove many to aspire to higher ranks and responsibilities within the crew.

- Privateering and Letters of Marque: Before turning to piracy, many sea rovers started as privateers, working under letters of marque issued by governments. These letters allowed them to legally target and capture ships of enemy nations. In return, the government would take a cut of the captured loot, while the privateers kept the rest. This was a state-sanctioned performance-based reward system, where better performance led to greater rewards.

- The Pirate "Constitution": Pirate captains like Bartholomew Roberts drafted codes or "constitutions" for their crew, outlining the division of plunder and compensation for injuries. For example, a pirate losing a limb in battle might receive a larger share of the loot as compensation. Such provisions ensured that pirates were motivated to fight bravely, knowing they'd be compensated for their risks.

In both the realms of piracy and business, performance-based rewards have proven to be a timeless motivator, driving individuals to achieve, innovate, and perform at their best.

2. Balancing Effort and Reward: Ensuring Fairness

The world of piracy, contrary to popular belief, wasn't just about chaos and lawlessness. There were codes, unwritten rules, and a deep sense of justice. When a pirate crew successfully plundered a ship, the loot wasn't just haphazardly divided. There was a system, often democratic, ensuring that each member got a share commensurate with their contribution. The captain, while getting a larger share, ensured that even the newest crew member was rewarded fairly. This sense of balance and fairness was crucial in maintaining morale, loyalty, and a sense of camaraderie among the pirates.

- **Transparency as a Pillar:** Just as pirates had clear codes outlining how loot would be divided, businesses should have transparent reward systems. Employees should understand how their efforts will be recognized and rewarded, eliminating ambiguities that can lead to dissatisfaction.

- **Fostering a Culture of Appreciation:** Beyond monetary rewards, a simple acknowledgment or expression of appreciation can go a long way. In the world of piracy, loyalty was often cemented not just by fair division of loot but also by mutual respect and camaraderie. Similarly, businesses can build loyalty by fostering a culture where employees feel valued.

- **Meritocracy in Practice:** The essence of fairness lies in ensuring that rewards are based on merit rather than favoritism or bias. Companies should strive to establish meritocratic practices, where individuals are judged based on their contributions rather than other irrelevant factors.

- **Feedback Loops:** Just as pirate crews often held meetings to discuss their strategies and share their concerns, businesses should have feedback mechanisms. Through regular check-ins and performance reviews, employees can understand where they stand and what they need to do to align better with the company's reward system.

- **The Role of Leadership:** The pirate captain played a pivotal role in ensuring fairness. In the corporate world, leaders, too, bear the responsibility of ensuring that the system is fair. They should be approachable, receptive to feedback, and proactive in addressing any disparities that arise.

- **The Broader Impact:** Fairness in rewards isn't just beneficial for individual employees; it impacts the entire organization. A fair system boosts morale, reduces turnover, and promotes a collaborative environment. It sends a clear message that the company values all its members and is committed to recognizing and nurturing talent at all levels.

In conclusion, the notion of balancing effort and reward is deeply rooted in the principles of justice, respect, and mutual benefit. Just as pirates thrived by ensuring every member felt valued, modern businesses can foster growth, loyalty, and innovation by embracing a culture of fairness. It's not just about equitably distributing profits; it's about building an environment where each individual feels recognized, valued, and motivated to give their best.

Figure 6- Midjourney(2023)

Drawing a parallel to the business realm, the concept of fairness in performance-based rewards is equally, if not more, crucial. In organizations, leaders must ensure that rewards are not just tied to results but also to effort. They must create systems that recognize both tangible achievements and the intangible efforts that employees put in. This balance ensures that while top performers are rewarded, those who show potential, and dedication are also recognized and motivated.

Real World Business Examples of "Balancing Effort and Reward: Ensuring Fairness":

- Performance Reviews and Peer Feedback: Many companies have moved away from traditional hierarchical performance reviews to 360-degree feedback systems. Here, employees receive feedback not just from superiors, but also from peers, subordinates, and sometimes even clients. This comprehensive feedback ensures that the complete range of an employee's contributions, including efforts that might not directly translate into results, is recognized.

- Team-based Bonuses: Some organizations offer team-based bonuses, where a team is collectively rewarded for achieving a goal. This recognizes that while individual contributions might vary, the combined effort of the team is what led to success. It ensures that individuals working behind the scenes, whose efforts might not be directly visible but are crucial for the project, are rewarded.

- Employee Recognition Programs: Beyond monetary rewards, many companies have instituted recognition programs where employees are acknowledged for various efforts – from innovation and collaboration to mentoring and community service. These programs ensure that employees feel valued for the diverse ways in which they contribute to the organization.

Historical Pirate Examples of "Balancing Effort and Reward: Ensuring Fairness":

- The Pirate Code: Many pirate ships operated under a "Pirate Code" or "Articles of Agreement". These documents, while varying from ship to ship, often had detailed provisions for the division of spoils. They ensured that shares were allocated based on rank and responsibility but also made provisions for injuries or disabilities sustained during raids, ensuring that pirates who took greater risks or suffered injuries were fairly compensated.

- Election of Pirate Captains: The captain of a pirate ship was often elected by the crew and could be deposed if he did not act in the crew's best interests. This democratic approach ensured that the captain, while enjoying certain privileges, was always answerable to the crew, creating a balance of power and ensuring fairness in decisions, including the division of loot. (Wikipedia, n.d.)

- Shared Ownership: Unlike naval ships or merchant vessels, where the ship was owned by a monarch or a rich merchant, pirate ships were often considered collective property. This sense of shared ownership meant that decisions, including those about the division of spoils, were made collectively, ensuring everyone's voice was heard and fairness was maintained.

In both piracy and modern business, the understanding that rewards should reflect effort and contribution, not just position or power, has been crucial in building cohesive, motivated, and effective teams.

3. Fostering Growth: Beyond Monetary Rewards

For many pirates, the allure of piracy wasn't just the promise of gold and jewels. It was also about the thrill of adventure, the promise of freedom, and the opportunity to rise through the ranks based on merit. Pirates like Calico Jack, who started as ordinary sailors, rose to become formidable captains because of their skills, cunning, and leadership abilities. In the world of piracy, growth wasn't just about accumulating wealth; it was also about gaining respect, authority, and influence.

Similarly, in modern businesses, performance-based rewards go beyond just monetary incentives. For many employees, growth opportunities, mentorship, training, and recognition are just as valuable, if not more so, than financial rewards. Leaders and organizations that recognize this are able to foster a culture of continuous learning, innovation, and loyalty. They understand that by investing in their employees' growth, they're not just rewarding past performance but also ensuring future successes.

Real World Business Examples of "Fostering Growth: Beyond Monetary Rewards":

- Google's 20% Time: Google famously had a policy where employees could use 20% of their work time on personal projects that they believed would benefit the company. This wasn't a direct financial reward, but it provided employees with the opportunity to pursue their passions, innovate, and contribute to the company in unique ways. Products like Gmail and Google News were the result of this initiative, showcasing the value of providing growth and creative opportunities beyond just monetary incentives. (Clark, 2022)

- Leadership Development Programs: Many multinational companies, like General Electric (GE) or Procter & Gamble (P&G), have structured leadership development or management trainee programs. These programs groom high-potential employees for leadership roles, offering them mentorship, cross-functional exposure, and international assignments. While these don't provide immediate financial rewards, they prepare employees for future leadership roles, showcasing a clear path of growth within the company.

- Recognition Programs: Companies like Microsoft and Salesforce have instituted recognition programs where employees are acknowledged and celebrated for various achievements – from product innovations to community service. Such recognition, often in the form of awards, events, or public acknowledgment, serves as a powerful motivator, signaling the company's appreciation and investment in their employees' growth and contributions.

Historical Pirate Examples of "Fostering Growth: Beyond Monetary Rewards":

- Mentorship and Apprenticeship: Young pirates, or "powder monkeys," were often taken under the wings of more experienced pirates, learning the ropes of seafaring, navigation, and combat. This mentorship wasn't a monetary reward, but it allowed these young pirates to acquire skills, knowledge, and eventually rise through the ranks, possibly even becoming captains themselves.

- Democratic Decision-Making: Pirate ships were often more democratic than other vessels of their time. Major decisions, from potential targets to division of loot, were put to a vote. This system allowed even the lowest-ranking pirates to have a say and feel a sense of ownership and influence, fostering a sense of growth and belonging.

- Codes of Conduct and Protection: The Pirate Codes or Articles of Agreement on many ships included provisions for injured pirates, ensuring they received a larger share or were taken care of. This system, while also serving as a form of insurance, demonstrated a commitment to the crew's well-being, fostering loyalty and a sense that the pirate life offered protection and long-term growth beyond just the immediate spoils of a raid.

Both in the world of pirates and modern businesses, understanding the multifaceted nature of rewards – going beyond just the financial and tapping into personal growth, recognition, and long-term development – has been crucial for sustained success and loyalty.

As we draw the curtains on this chapter, it's essential to pause and reflect on the profound insights that the pirate code "No Prey, No Pay" offers to the modern business world. At its core, this principle underscores the age-old connection between effort and reward, between risk and return. It serves as a poignant reminder that in any venture, be it on the high seas or in the corporate boardrooms, rewards are seldom handed on a silver platter. They must be earned, often through a combination of skill, strategy, and sheer determination. But as we've seen, it's not just about the act of taking or achieving; it's about doing so with fairness, integrity, and a keen sense of responsibility.

Figure 7- Midjourney(2023)

In the world of piracy, where danger lurked around every corner and every voyage was fraught with uncertainty, the promise of reward served as a beacon, guiding pirates through their most challenging moments. It motivated them to collaborate, to innovate, and to push their boundaries. But alongside this drive, there was also an unwritten code of honor, a sense of justice that ensured that rewards were distributed fairly, that every member of the crew, regardless of their rank or role, was recognized for their contribution. This delicate balance between ambition and fairness is something that modern businesses can draw inspiration from.

Furthermore, as leaders and organizations navigate the complex waters of performance-based rewards, they must also recognize the broader implications of their reward systems. It's not just about motivating employees or driving results; it's about fostering a culture of growth, recognition, and continuous learning. It's about understanding that while monetary rewards are important, they are just one piece of the puzzle. True, lasting motivation comes from recognizing and nurturing potential, from offering opportunities for growth, and from creating an environment where every individual feels valued and empowered.

In the words of Captain Martin Marlinspike, "The seas of business are vast and unpredictable, but with the right compass of fairness, recognition, and growth, one can navigate through the most challenging storms and reach the shores of success." As we anchor this chapter and look to the horizon, may the lessons from the world of piracy guide your sails, and may your journey be as rewarding as the destination.

Chapter 5: "Navigating Uncharted Waters" - Embracing Uncertainty in the Business Realm

Aaaarrrrgggghhhh!, my corporate adventurers and desk-bound buccaneers! 'Tis the voice of Captain Martin Marlinspike, First Mate of the ship 'Entrepreneur's Endeavor', speaking to your ambitious souls. With a twirl of my ruffled skirt, a sparkle in my discerning eye, and the brisk wind of tales from high seas adventures blowing through my fiery, untamed hair, I'm here to share the secrets and stories that have steered me well, both on the boundless ocean and in the world of commerce.

From where ye stand, atop the towering decks of your own endeavors, the business landscape might appear a wild, unpredictable ocean, where treacherous storms can brew without warning, and where unseen opportunities lurk beneath the surface, waiting to be discovered by the keenest of eyes. And ye'd be right. But fret not, for this chapter isn't about instilling fear, but about arming ye with the right weapons and wit to face those challenges head-on.

For every swashbuckler, whether of the sea or the boardroom, the heart of the matter remains the same: How does one navigate the unknown? How can ye plot a course through waters where no charts exist? Just as we pirates must often rely on starlight, instinct, and the whispers of the winds, so too must business leaders learn to decipher the subtle cues of the market, trusting in their teams, their experience, and sometimes, their gut feelings.

Figure 8- Midjourney(2023)

1. Embracing the Unknown: The Courage to Venture

In the vast expanse of the seas, with nothing but the horizon in sight, pirates sailed fearlessly. Their journeys were fraught with uncertainties – storms, hostile territories, and unseen dangers lurking below the water. Yet, the allure of the unknown, the possibility of unearthing riches, and the thrill of discovery propelled them forward.

Their stories, filled with legendary voyages and daring exploits, stand testament to their indomitable spirit and appetite for risk.

Much like the seas, today's business environment is unpredictable and ever evolving. Just as pirates navigated through treacherous waters, businesses must navigate through economic downturns, disruptive technologies, and shifting market dynamics. The challenges might be different, but the underlying principle remains the same: the ability to face the unknown head-on.

- **Adaptive Innovation:** Just as pirates had to adapt their strategies based on new maps, information, or tools available to them, businesses must also continuously innovate to stay relevant. Companies like Nokia and Kodak, once giants in their respective fields, faltered because they were unable to adapt to the rapidly changing tech landscape. On the other hand, companies like Apple and Amazon have thrived by continuously reinventing themselves, showing an insatiable curiosity for what lies ahead.

- **Calculated Risks**: Every decision a pirate made, from attacking a ship to anchoring in a cove, was a gamble. Similarly, in business, every investment, merger, or strategy shift carries an inherent risk. But as with piracy, it's not about avoiding risks but calculating them. Successful companies evaluate potential challenges and rewards, making informed decisions that can lead to exponential growth.

- **Embracing Diversity:** Pirates often formed crews from diverse backgrounds, understanding that different perspectives and experiences could offer unique solutions to challenges faced at sea. Today, businesses recognize the value of diverse teams. Different backgrounds bring different viewpoints, leading to innovative solutions and creative problem-solving.

- **Continuous Learning:** The sea was a harsh teacher, and pirates had to learn from their mistakes quickly. Mistakes were costly, sometimes even fatal. In the world of business, the market is that unforgiving teacher. Companies that foster a culture of continuous learning and are quick to adapt from their missteps often stay ahead of the curve.

- **The Spirit of Exploration:** At the heart of piracy was the spirit of exploration, a deep-rooted desire to discover what's beyond the known. In business, this translates to exploring new markets, experimenting with unconventional ideas, and not being afraid to venture outside the comfort zone. Companies that embody this spirit, like SpaceX with its quest for space exploration or Google with its numerous 'moonshot' projects, push the boundaries of what's possible.

In essence, the stories of pirates, with their audacious courage and insatiable curiosity, serve as a metaphor for businesses in today's volatile world. It reminds us that embracing the unknown, while challenging, can lead to untapped opportunities, groundbreaking innovations, and lasting success.

Real World Business Examples of "Embracing the Unknown: The Courage to Venture":

- Apple's Entry into Mobile Phones: When Apple decided to venture into the mobile phone market with the iPhone in 2007, it was treading into unknown territory. They were taking on industry giants like Nokia and BlackBerry. However, their courage to innovate and redefine what a smartphone could be turned the industry on its head and solidified Apple's position as a market leader. (Frommer, 2011)

- Netflix's Shift from DVDs to Streaming: Netflix started as a DVD rental-by-mail service, challenging traditional video rental stores. But they didn't stop there. Seeing the potential of the internet and changing consumer behavior, they made a bold move to pivot towards online streaming, an area that was largely uncharted at the time. This daring venture into the unknown made Netflix a dominant player in the entertainment industry. (Gibbons, 2019)

- SpaceX's Reusable Rockets: The aerospace industry, for the longest time, had accepted that rocket boosters were single-use. Elon Musk's SpaceX challenged this norm by aiming for, and achieving, reusable rocket boosters. Despite many doubters and the inherent risks of space exploration, SpaceX's courage to venture into this unknown paved the way for more sustainable and cost-effective space travel. (Thompson, 2018)

Historical Pirate Examples of "Embracing the Unknown: The Courage to Venture":

- Black Bart's Atlantic and Indian Ocean Raids: Bartholomew Roberts, also known as Black Bart, was one of the most successful pirates of his time. Not content with just the Caribbean, he expanded his raids into the Atlantic and even ventured into the Indian Ocean. His willingness to explore unknown waters and take on unfamiliar foes made him one of the most feared pirates of his era.

- Captain Kidd's Expedition to the Indian Ocean: Originally commissioned as a privateer to hunt pirates, Captain William Kidd chose to turn pirate himself, venturing into the lesser-known waters of the Indian Ocean for western pirates. This bold move into uncharted territory might not have ended well for Kidd personally, but it showcased the pirate spirit of embracing the unknown.

- **Anne Bonny and Mary Read Breaking Gender Norms:** In an era where piracy was a male-dominated profession, Anne Bonny and Mary Read broke gender barriers to become two of the most notorious pirates on the Caribbean seas. Embracing the unknown, they took on roles traditionally reserved for men, challenging societal norms and proving their mettle in the process.

Whether on the high seas or in boardrooms, the courage to step into the unknown, to challenge the status quo, and to embrace change has been a defining factor for those who leave a lasting mark in their respective domains.

2. Adaptability: The Pirate's Compass

Adaptability, for pirates, was not just a virtue; it was a necessity. Every day on the high seas presented new challenges – unexpected storms, encounters with rival pirates, or unforeseen obstacles like treacherous rocks and reefs. Their environment was dynamic, and so they had to be as well. Their tales of survival, quick thinking, and course correction provide invaluable insights for businesses today.

- **Lessons from Nature:** Just as pirates learned to read the skies and the seas for signs of changing weather, businesses need to be attuned to the shifting signals in their industries. Early detection of change – be it a trend in consumer behavior, a new technological development, or a change in regulatory policies – allows for timely response and adjustment. Netflix, for instance, read the winds of change and pivoted from a DVD rental model to a streaming service, ensuring its dominance in the entertainment sector.

- **Resilience in the Face of Setbacks:** Pirates often encountered setbacks, be it the loss of crew members, ship damages, or empty treasure hunts. However, they pressed on, adapting their strategies and learning from their mistakes. Similarly, companies will face challenges, but it's their ability to bounce back and adapt that defines their long-term success. Toyota's rapid recovery after the 2011 tsunami in Japan by streamlining its supply chain is a testament to this adaptability.

- **Embracing Diverse Thought:** Pirate crews were often composed of individuals from different backgrounds, cultures, and experiences. This diversity fostered a multitude of solutions to any given problem. Today's businesses thrive on diversity and inclusion, understanding that diverse teams bring a range of perspectives, leading to innovative solutions and adaptability to change.

- **Continuous Skill Development**: The best pirates were also the best learners. They had to continuously refine their skills – from navigation to combat – to stay ahead of rivals and the navy. Businesses today need to invest in continuous learning and development for their teams. In a rapidly evolving world, skills can become obsolete quickly. Companies like Microsoft and Adobe, for example, have shifted to continuous learning models, ensuring their teams are always equipped with the latest skills.

Figure 9- Midjourney(2023)

- **Flexibility in Strategy:** The seas taught pirates to be flexible. If a planned route was fraught with danger, they quickly devised a new one. In the business world, while long-term strategies are essential, there needs to be flexibility in execution. Take the case of Slack, which started as a gaming company but pivoted to become a leading communication platform when its founders saw a more significant opportunity there.

In the unpredictable waters of the business world, adaptability is the compass that can guide companies through uncertainty. It's not just about reacting to change but proactively embracing and leveraging it. As the pirates of old knew all too well, those who adapt, survive, and thrive.

Real World Business Examples of "Adaptability: The Pirate's Compass":

- Nokia's Shift from Paper to Phones: Before becoming known as a mobile phone giant, Nokia began its journey in the 19th century as a pulp mill company, manufacturing paper products. Over the years, they ventured into various industries including rubber, cables, and electronics. It was their adaptability that allowed them to eventually focus on telecommunications and introduce some of the most iconic mobile phones in history.

- Adobe's Transition to Subscription Models: Adobe, once known primarily for its boxed software products, recognized the changing dynamics of the software market and the rising cloud-based solutions. They took a bold step to transition their entire software suite to a subscription-based model, Adobe Creative Cloud, effectively transforming their revenue model and adapting to modern consumer preferences.

- Kodak's Evolution in Imaging: Although famously known for missing the digital photography revolution initially, Kodak, after facing bankruptcy, has been trying to reinvent itself. From its roots in film photography, Kodak has since diversified into areas like digital printing and even explored blockchain technology for image rights management. (Clay, 2020)

Historical Pirate Examples of "Adaptability: The Pirate's Compass":

- Pirates Turning Privateers and Vice Versa: Throughout history, many pirates became privateers (state-sanctioned pirates) when offered the opportunity, and conversely, many privateers turned pirates when circumstances changed. Their ability to shift roles based on political climates showcased their adaptability.

- Use of the Jolly Roger: Pirates often adapted their flags, or Jolly Rogers, to instill specific fears. While the classic skull and crossbones is well-known, pirates would modify and customize their flags based on their targets, sending different messages and adapting their psychological warfare tactics.

- Pirates' Diverse Ships: Pirates didn't always have a specific type of ship. They would often capture and adapt various vessels to suit their needs, making modifications to increase speed or firepower. This flexibility allowed them to be more versatile and unpredictable in their operations.

Adaptability, whether on the high seas or in the corporate landscape, requires an openness to change, a willingness to learn, and the agility to act. It ensures that one remains relevant, competitive, and ahead of the curve, regardless of the challenges ahead.

3. Continuous Learning: Charting New Courses

In the age of sail, pirates couldn't rely solely on old maps and past experiences. The very nature of their profession forced them to be adaptable and quick learners. They were not just navigators of the seas but navigators of information, always gathering, assessing, and applying new knowledge. This dedication to continuous learning mirrors what is needed in today's fast-paced business environment.

- **Learning from Experience:** Pirates often operated based on trial and error. An encounter with a heavily fortified ship might mean developing new tactics or a shipwreck could lead to a better understanding of treacherous waters. Similarly, businesses must see setbacks not as failures but as learning opportunities. Organizations like Amazon, which emphasizes its willingness to fail in pursuit of innovation, highlight this approach.

- **Cross-pollination of Ideas:** The pirate world was a melting pot of cultures and backgrounds. African rhythms, European melodies, and Caribbean beats mixed to create sea shanties. This sharing of knowledge across diverse groups led to richer solutions and innovations. Today's businesses recognize this, with companies like Google encouraging cross-departmental collaboration to foster innovation.

- **Staying Ahead of the Curve:** Pirates had to be aware of technological advances such as improvements in ship design or navigation tools. Those who didn't keep up found themselves at a disadvantage. Likewise, businesses today must remain updated with the latest in tech, market trends, and industry shifts. Companies like Apple, which consistently reinvent their product lines, demonstrate the power of staying ahead.

- **Investing in Training:** Pirates had to train constantly, honing their skills in combat, navigation, and other essential areas. Today, businesses must invest in their employees' growth and training. Companies like Salesforce, with their Trailhead platform, are dedicated to upskilling their workforce, ensuring they remain competitive and effective.

Figure 10- Midjourney(2023)

- **Embracing External Sources of Knowledge:** Pirates weren't shy about learning from other cultures or even from their adversaries. They would incorporate techniques from the navies they fought against or from the merchants they plundered. Businesses today similarly recognize the value in learning from competitors, from attending industry conferences, or from benchmarking studies, ensuring they gain a broader perspective.

Continuous learning is not just a modern business mantra; it's a timeless principle, as demonstrated by the pirates of yesteryears. It's about recognizing that the world is in constant flux and that to navigate this changing landscape effectively, one must always be willing to learn, adapt, and chart new courses.

Real World Business Examples of "Continuous Learning: Charting New Courses":

- Google's Foray into Different Domains: Starting as a search engine company, Google continuously learned and ventured into various sectors, including smartphones (Pixel), cloud computing (Google Cloud), AI, and autonomous vehicles (Waymo). Their ability to expand stems from a commitment to continuous learning and R&D. (Verge, 2018)

- Amazon's Evolution: Beginning as an online bookstore, Amazon learned, adapted, and expanded into diverse sectors: e-commerce, cloud computing (AWS), streaming (Amazon Prime), and even physical retail (Whole Foods acquisition). Their willingness to explore new domains and learn has made them a global giant. (DePillis & Sherman, 2018)

- Microsoft's Transformation: After dominating the PC software market with Windows, Microsoft faced challenges with the rise of mobile computing. Under the leadership of Satya Nadella, Microsoft embraced a learning mindset, focusing on cloud computing (Azure), acquiring LinkedIn, and innovating in AI and augmented reality. (Tabrizi, 2023)

Historical Pirate Examples of "Continuous Learning: Charting New Courses":

- Navigation Techniques: Pirates were among the earliest adopters of advanced navigation techniques, tools, and maps.

They were known to learn and employ the latest navigational methods, like the use of astrolabes, to chart new courses and discover unexplored territories.

- Ship Adaptations: Pirates continuously updated their ships for better performance. This involved learning about various ship designs and incorporating features that would make their vessels faster, more maneuverable, or more heavily armed depending on their requirements.

- Multilingualism Among Pirates: Given that they interacted with various cultures across different ports and targeted ships from different nations, many pirates learned multiple languages. This skill not only helped in communication but also in understanding and strategizing based on their victims' plans and conversations.

In both piracy and business, the landscape is ever-changing. Those who commit to continuous learning ensure that they are not only prepared for the challenges of today but are also equipped to seize the opportunities of tomorrow.

4. Preparedness: The Pirate's Arsenal

While pirates were known for their audacity and spontaneity, they always ensured they were prepared for whatever the seas threw at them. Their ships were stocked with provisions, their crews were trained for battles, and they always had a plan (or two) up their sleeves. In the world of business, while it's essential to be agile and spontaneous, it's equally crucial to be prepared for the uncertainties that lie ahead. This means having contingency plans in place, being proactive rather than reactive, and always being a step ahead of the competition. It's about foreseeing potential challenges, having strategies to overcome them, and ensuring that when the storm hits, you're not just ready to weather it, but to harness it to your advantage.

The mythos of pirates paints them as carefree and reckless, but in reality, they operated on principles that often intersect with successful business strategies. One such principle is preparedness, and here's how it unfolded in both the pirate realm and modern business:

- **Risk Assessment:** Before embarking on a voyage, pirates would often gauge the potential risks – from adverse weather conditions to potential confrontations with navy vessels. Similarly, businesses conduct SWOT analyses (Strengths, Weaknesses, Opportunities, Threats) before launching products or entering new markets. By understanding potential vulnerabilities and threats, companies can better strategize to mitigate risks.

- **Resource Management:** Pirates ensured their ships were equipped with adequate food, fresh water, weapons, and other essentials. They also ensured they had the manpower needed for both sailing and potential confrontations. In business, resource allocation – be it finances, manpower, or technology – and ensuring there's enough buffer to handle unforeseen circumstances is crucial. Companies like Toyota, with their Just-in-Time inventory system, exemplify efficient resource management. (Shih, 2022)

- **Versatility of Skills:** On a pirate ship, every crew member had a primary role but was also cross-trained in other tasks. This ensured that the ship could function even if some members were incapacitated. Modern businesses emphasize cross-training and upskilling, ensuring that operations continue smoothly even in the face of disruptions. Tech giants like

Microsoft often rotate roles within teams to promote skill versatility.

- **Scenario Planning:** Pirates didn't just have Plan A; they often had a Plan B and C. If an attack strategy failed, they would quickly switch to another. Today, businesses use scenario planning to envision various futures and devise strategies for each. This ensures they aren't caught off-guard. For instance, Shell Oil Company is renowned for its extensive scenario planning, which helped it navigate various oil crises.

- **Embracing Innovation:** Pirates were quick to adopt new technologies, be it advanced navigational tools or better ship designs, ensuring they had the upper hand. In the corporate world, early adoption of emerging technologies can offer a competitive edge. Companies like Netflix pivoted from DVD rentals to streaming, capitalizing on technological advancements. (Gibbons, 2019)

- **Continuous Monitoring:** Pirates often had lookouts, keeping an eye out for potential threats or opportunities, be it an approaching storm or a merchant ship laden with treasures. Similarly, businesses today invest in market research and monitoring tools to stay updated on industry trends and competitor moves.

In both piracy and business, preparedness isn't just about avoiding pitfalls; it's about ensuring you're in the best position to capitalize on opportunities and navigate challenges. It's about being equipped, both in resources and strategy, to sail confidently into the future.

Real World Business Examples of "Preparedness: The Pirate's Arsenal":

- Apple's Supply Chain Mastery: Apple, the tech giant, has been lauded for its efficient and robust supply chain management. They ensure preparedness by maintaining relationships with multiple suppliers, predicting potential component shortages, and securing necessary parts well in advance to meet product launch deadlines. (Ross & Naoum, 2023)

- Toyota's Production System (TPS): Toyota is well-known for its Just-In-Time (JIT) production methodology, which ensures that parts arrive just when they're needed. But they also prioritize the principle of *jidoka*, which means any employee in the production line can stop the process if there's a quality issue, ensuring that problems are addressed immediately and don't escalate. (Shih, 2022)

- Netflix's Content Diversification: As streaming wars intensified, Netflix prepared for the potential loss of third-party content by investing billions in original content. They foresaw major studios pulling content for their platforms and strategically built a vast library of Netflix Originals to retain subscribers. (Gibbons, 2019)

Historical Pirate Examples of "Preparedness: The Pirate's Arsenal":

- Blackbeard's Fearsome Reputation: Blackbeard, also known as Edward Teach, cultivated a terrifying image. He lit slow-burning fuses in his beard during battles, creating a demonic appearance. This psychological warfare tactic ensured that many ships surrendered without a fight. Though it was a show, it showcased his preparedness to strike fear into his enemies.

- Bartolomeu Português's Escape Plans: The notorious pirate was known for his cunning escape plans. When captured in

Campeche in 1663, he had already prepared a getaway. With the help of some allies, he escaped from prison, proving that a pirate always had backup plans ready. (Álvarez, 2020)

- Anne Bonny and Mary Read's Disguise: These two female pirates often dressed as men, not only to fit into the pirate world but also as a strategic move. When confronted, their unsuspecting enemies often found themselves outmatched. Their preparedness in maintaining such disguises provided them an advantage in surprise and tactics.

Both in the turbulent waters of the seas and the equally challenging waves of the business world, preparedness ensures not just survival but a significant advantage against adversaries.

As we drop anchor on this chapter, let's take a moment to reflect on the vast, unpredictable seas of business. Much like the pirates of old, who faced the vastness of the ocean with courage, cunning, and a touch of audacity, businesses today must navigate the ever-changing waters of the market with adaptability, foresight, and a thirst for continuous learning. Embracing uncertainty doesn't mean venturing forth blindly; it means being prepared, staying informed, and having the courage to face the unknown. In the grand tapestry of business, it's often the intangible traits - the courage to venture, the ability to adapt, the commitment to continuous learning, and the preparedness for the unknown - that determine success. These are the traits that set leaders apart, that transform challenges into opportunities, and that ensure long-term success in the tumultuous seas of business. So, as you chart your course in the corporate world, remember to embrace the unknown, to adapt, to learn, and to

Figure 11- Midjourney(2023)

always be prepared. For in the unpredictable seas of business, as in the thrilling tales of piracy, it's often the journey that teaches you the most. Every challenge, every change, and every uncertainty is an opportunity to learn, adapt, and grow. And as Captain Martin Marlinspike would say, "In the grand adventure of business, it's not the destination but the voyage that truly counts." So, hoist your sails, chart your course, and embrace the adventure that lies ahead. May your journey be filled with discoveries, successes, and a touch of pirate flair. Until our next tale, sail boldly and prosper, my darlings!

Chapter 6: "Dead Men Tell No Tales" - The Importance of Secrecy and Discretion in Business

Yo Ho Yo Ho!, fellow seekers of wisdom! As we navigate the uncharted waters of business, guided by the captivating tales of pirates, we find ourselves entering a realm where words hold immense power - the realm of effective communication. The world of piracy, with its legends of hidden treasures, daring escapades, and infamous pirate crews, has always beckoned with a sense of intrigue. But beyond the swashbuckling adventures and epic battles, there lies a lesson that transcends time: the power of words to shape destinies, forge alliances, and lead to both triumph and ruin. It's this lesson, drawn from the tales of pirates and their code of communication, that we shall unravel in this chapter.

In the tumultuous era of piracy, where every encounter was a potential battle, effective communication was the cornerstone of survival. Pirates, whether issuing commands during a raid or negotiating alliances, had to convey their intentions with precision and clarity. The wrong word, a misunderstood signal, or a poorly delivered message could spell disaster. Hence, the phrase "Dead Men Tell No Tales" held particular significance. It served as a stark reminder of the consequences of miscommunication. This world, where information traveled not at the speed of light but through words, symbols, and actions, underscores the timeless importance of communication in every endeavor.

Now, one might question how the world of pirates, with its crude methods of communication, relates to the modern business arena, characterized by emails, video conferences, and social media. The answer lies in the essence of effective communication, which transcends the medium. In the competitive landscape of business, where decisions are made in split seconds and collaborations span continents, the ability to convey ideas clearly, to listen attentively, and to understand beyond the spoken word is paramount. The most successful leaders and entrepreneurs are those who recognize that communication is not just about the words spoken but also about the emotions conveyed, the context understood, and the connections forged.

So, as we delve into this chapter, let us channel the lessons of the pirate crews and their code of communication. Let us explore the intricacies of effective communication, both verbal and nonverbal, and its impact on building relationships, fostering collaboration, and achieving shared objectives. Join me, dear reader, on this voyage to uncover the secrets of how words, like the winds, can propel us forward or steer us off course. Together, we shall unravel the art of communication, drawing inspiration from the legends of pirates and applying their timeless wisdom to the challenges and opportunities of the modern business world.

1. Guarding the Treasure: Protecting Intellectual Property

In the world of business, intellectual property (IP) is akin to the coveted treasure maps of pirate lore. These maps, often marked with an 'X' to denote the treasure's location, were fiercely guarded by

Figure 12- Midjourney(2023)

pirates, for they held the promise of untold riches. Similarly, IP represents the innovative spirit, hard work, and investment of a company. It's the blueprint of their success, the roadmap to their future endeavors. Protecting this IP is not just about legal rights; it's about safeguarding a company's future, its competitive edge, and its reputation in the market. In an era where imitation is rampant and competition is fierce, companies that fail to protect their IP risk losing their competitive advantage, their market share, and even their very existence. Just as a pirate would go to great lengths to protect their treasure map, even if it meant swallowing it to prevent it from falling into enemy hands, businesses must be vigilant in protecting their IP from prying eyes and potential threats.

Real World Business Examples of "Guarding the Treasure: Protecting Intellectual Property":

- Apple vs. Samsung Patent Wars: Apple has consistently defended its intellectual property rights. One of the most high-profile instances was its prolonged legal battle with Samsung over patent infringements related to the design and functionality of their smartphones. The lawsuit, spanning multiple countries, underscored the lengths to which companies would go to protect their IP. (Kastrenakes, 2018)

- Disney's Copyright Extensions: The Walt Disney Company is known for its aggressive protection of its intellectual properties. Over the years, Disney has played a significant role in pushing for copyright extensions in the U.S., ensuring their beloved characters and stories remain under their control for extended periods. (Lee, 2013)

- Qualcomm's Licensing Model: Qualcomm, a major player in the semiconductor and telecommunications industry, has a significant portion of its revenues coming from licensing its vast IP portfolio related to wireless communication technologies. Their aggressive stance on IP protection has led to various legal battles over licensing terms and conditions. (Eassa, 2019)

Historical Pirate Examples of "Guarding the Treasure: Protecting Intellectual Property":

- Captain Kidd's Buried Treasure: Captain William Kidd was one of the few pirates known to have buried his treasure.

Realizing the value of his loot and fearing it would be taken, Kidd buried a portion of his treasure on Gardiners Island. This act was an early form of "protecting" his valuable assets from potential threats.

- Pirate Codes and Secrets: Pirates, like Bartholomew Roberts, often had a code of conduct or articles that the crew would agree upon. These were closely guarded secrets, much like modern IP, ensuring that the pirate crew had a competitive edge over their adversaries. These codes defined shares, behavior, and consequences, creating a sense of order amidst the lawlessness.

- Map and Route Protection: Pirate captains, aware of the value of their navigational knowledge, would often keep secret routes, hideouts, and safe passages close to their chests. They'd avoid sharing detailed maps openly, ensuring that such invaluable knowledge didn't fall into competitors' or enemies' hands.

Both in the cutthroat world of piracy and the competitive realm of modern business, guarding one's most prized assets, be it tangible treasure or intangible intellectual property, remains a top priority.

2. The Art of Strategic Silence: Knowing When to Hold Your Tongue

Silence, as they say, is golden. In the treacherous world of piracy, a loose tongue could lead to a swift end, be it through betrayal, mutiny, or capture by the enemy. Pirates knew the value of strategic silence, understanding that sometimes, what you don't say is more powerful than what you do. In the realm of business, this principle holds true. Companies often find themselves in situations where revealing too much can jeopardize their position, be it during a negotiation, a product launch, or even a corporate merger. By holding back, by maintaining an air of mystery, they can control the narrative, keep competitors guessing, and create a buzz that can be leveraged to their advantage. Strategic silence can also be a tool for damage control, allowing companies to regroup, reassess, and respond with a well-thought-out strategy rather than a knee-jerk reaction. In essence, knowing when to speak and when to hold one's tongue can be the difference between success and failure in the cutthroat world of business.

Figure 13 - Midjourney(2023)

Real World Business Examples of "The Art of Strategic Silence: Knowing When to Hold Your Tongue":

- Apple's Product Launches: Apple is renowned for its culture of secrecy surrounding new product launches. By limiting leaks and maintaining strategic silence about the details of their upcoming products, Apple creates anticipation and buzz, ensuring that when they finally unveil a new product, it garners maximum attention. (Sullivan, 2017)

- Tesla's Elon Musk: Although Elon Musk is known for his vocal presence on social media platforms like Twitter, there have been strategic moments where he has remained silent or vague about certain aspects of his companies, allowing rumors to build anticipation or diverting attention away from potential negative news.

- Merger and Acquisition Negotiations: Many businesses maintain a policy of not commenting on "rumor or speculation" when questioned about potential mergers or acquisitions. This strategic silence allows them to conduct negotiations behind closed doors without external pressures or premature evaluations from the market or competitors.

Historical Pirate Examples of "The Art of Strategic Silence: Knowing When to Hold Your Tongue":

- Blackbeard's Intimidation Tactics: Legend has it that Blackbeard would light fuses in his beard to create an aura of menace and fear without having to say a word. This kind of silence, paired with theatrical intimidation, often meant that he didn't have to resort to violence as ships would surrender without a fight.

- Pirate's Marooning: Pirates would sometimes maroon individuals, essentially stranding them on uninhabited islands as a form of punishment or to keep secrets. This ensured that certain knowledge, plans, or betrayals remained hidden, using silence (or isolation) as a tool for control.

- Captain Kidd's Treasure Map: As previously mentioned with Captain Kidd, after burying his treasure, he refrained from revealing its location, even after his capture. His silence led to numerous legends and myths about the location of his buried treasure, with many still speculating about it today.

In both piracy and business, the power of silence, whether used for intrigue, strategy, or control, plays an integral role in shaping outcomes and narratives.

3. Navigating the Rumor Seas: Managing Information Flow

The high seas were rife with tales of ghost ships, cursed treasures, and mythical creatures. These tales, whispered from one sailor to another, could inspire hope, instill fear, or lead astray. Pirates had to be discerning, sifting through these tales to separate fact from fiction. Similarly, in today's digital age, businesses are inundated with a deluge of information. Rumors, speculations, and misinformation can spread like wildfire, thanks to the power of social media and the internet. Companies must be adept at navigating these rumor seas, managing the flow of information to ensure that their brand image remains untainted. This involves proactive communication, transparency, and sometimes, even damage control. By effectively managing information flow, companies can steer their ship through turbulent waters, ensuring that they remain on course and that their reputation remains intact.

- **The Double-Edged Sword of Digital Communication**: While the digital age has facilitated faster communication and broader outreach, it has also amplified the speed at which rumors spread. Just as a whisper about a ghost ship could create ripples across the seas, a single tweet or post can quickly snowball into a global narrative.

- **Tools for Detection:** Just as pirates had their compasses and maps to navigate, businesses can employ modern tools like sentiment analysis, media monitoring, and data analytics. These tools can help detect emerging narratives, allowing businesses to address them early on.

- **The Role of an Informed Crew:** Within a pirate crew, experienced sailors could often differentiate between mere myths and credible information. Similarly, an informed and educated workforce can act as a company's first line of defense against misinformation. When employees are kept in the loop and understand the company's vision and values, they can counteract false narratives and champion the brand's genuine story.

- **Crisis Communication:** At times, even the most skilled pirates faced storms they hadn't anticipated. Likewise, despite best efforts, companies might find themselves in the eye of a PR storm. Having a crisis communication plan in place ensures that companies can address issues head-on, clarify misunderstandings, and restore their reputation.

- **Authentic Engagement:** Engaging authentically with audiences can prevent the spread of rumors. Companies that maintain an active presence on social platforms, respond to queries, and address concerns in real-time can often nip potential issues in the bud.

- **Learning from the Tales:** Just as pirates would sometimes find grains of truth in the grand tales of the seas, businesses can glean insights from the narratives that surround them—even the false ones. Listening to these stories can provide companies with valuable feedback, helping them understand underlying concerns or perceptions that need addressing.

- **Setting the Narrative:** Rather than always being reactive, companies can also take a proactive stance by setting their own narratives. Sharing success stories, corporate values, and positive testimonials can create a buffer against negative rumors.

In essence, navigating the rumor seas is a complex endeavor that requires vigilance, adaptability, and foresight. In the face of ever-evolving narratives, businesses must be adept sailors, equipped with the right tools and strategies to chart a clear course and safeguard their reputation amidst the swirling maelstrom of information.

Real World Business Examples of "Navigating the Rumor Seas: Managing Information Flow":

- PepsiCo and the 'Needle in the Can' Rumor (1993): A false rumor spread rapidly that syringes and needles were being found in Pepsi cans. PepsiCo swiftly responded by collaborating with the FDA to confirm the rumor was baseless, releasing videos showing their canning process, and conducting press conferences. Their prompt and transparent response quelled the rumor and helped protect their brand image. (Newsweek, 1993)

- Starbucks and the 'War on Christmas' Controversy (2015): When Starbucks released a plain red holiday cup, it led to a social media storm with accusations that the company was waging a "war on Christmas". Starbucks navigated the situation by clarifying their intent was to embrace simplicity and inclusivity. (CBS News, 2015)

- KFC and the 'Mutant Chicken' Rumor: A rumor that KFC used genetically mutated chickens spread widely. KFC addressed this by launching a PR campaign that dispelled the myths and emphasized the quality of their chicken. They combined facts with humor and addressed the misinformation head-on. (Peterson, 2016)

Historical Pirate Examples of "Navigating the Rumor Seas: Managing Information Flow":

- Black Bart's Gentleman Pirate Image: Bartholomew Roberts, known as Black Bart, was one of the most successful pirates, yet he didn't drink alcohol and insisted on discipline and proper conduct aboard his ship. While pirates were generally considered ruthless, the rumors of a 'gentleman pirate' like Black Bart might have contributed to his success by making potential victims more likely to surrender without a fight, thinking they would be treated well.

- Anne Bonny and Mary Read Disguising as Men: To survive in the male-dominated world of piracy, Anne Bonny and Mary Read spread rumors and tales of their escapades as male pirates. By navigating and perpetuating these tales, they were able to earn respect and secure their place in pirate lore.

- Captain Kidd's Rumored Treasure: After being captured, tales of Captain Kidd's vast hidden treasure spread far and wide. Whether Kidd intentionally allowed these tales to spread to buy time or to maintain a certain reputation is unclear, but the rumors of his treasure persist to this day, making him one of history's most legendary pirates.

Both in the age of piracy and in the modern business world, managing information flow, addressing rumors, and ensuring that the right narrative prevails is crucial to maintain reputation and trust.

4. The Fortress of Discretion: Building Trust and Loyalty

Trust is a cornerstone of any relationship, be it between pirates on a ship or between a company and its stakeholders. In the world of piracy, betrayal was a grave offense, often met with dire consequences. Pirates relied on trust to function as a cohesive unit, to plan their raids, and to share their spoils. Any breach of this trust could lead to mutiny or worse. Similarly, in business, trust is paramount. Companies must build and maintain trust with their employees, partners, customers, and investors. This trust is built over time, through consistent actions, transparent communication, and discretion. Companies that are known to be discreet, that honor their commitments, and that protect sensitive information are often viewed more favorably by their stakeholders. In essence, discretion is a fortress that protects a company's most valuable asset: its reputation.

- **Actions Speak Louder:** While promises and grand gestures can be impactful, it's the consistent, day-to-day actions of a company that truly cement trust. Whether it's delivering products on time, maintaining quality, or ensuring data privacy, these consistent acts of integrity build a lasting trust.

- **The Currency of Discretion:** In the clandestine world of piracy, secrets were powerful. The same holds true in the business world. Companies that show discretion, especially when handling sensitive information about clients, partners, or employees, earn a reputation for reliability.

- **Transparency and Openness:** While discretion is crucial, it shouldn't be confused with opaqueness. Being open about business practices, challenges, and decisions can foster trust. Stakeholders value businesses that don't hide behind closed doors, but instead engage in open dialogue.

- **Reputation as an Asset:** Just as a pirate's reputation could ensure safe passage or instigate immediate conflict, a company's reputation plays a pivotal role in its business ventures. A reputation built on trust and loyalty can lead to increased brand loyalty, better partnerships, and a competitive edge in the market.

- **Handling Breaches:** No crew is immune to betrayal, just as no company is impervious to mistakes. What differentiates great leaders from the rest is how they handle these breaches. Addressing issues head-on, making amends, and ensuring accountability can actually strengthen trust in the long run.

- **Rewarding Loyalty:** Pirates often had codes for sharing spoils, ensuring that loyalty and hard work were rewarded. In the corporate world, recognizing and rewarding stakeholder loyalty, whether it's through customer loyalty programs, employee incentives, or investor dividends, reinforces trust and encourages continued allegiance.

- **Continuous Cultivation:** Trust isn't a one-time achievement; it's a continuous endeavor. Like the walls of a fortress that need regular maintenance to withstand assaults, the trust a company builds needs constant nurturing. Regular engagement, open communication, and consistent ethical behavior are the bricks and mortar of this fortress of discretion.

In the volatile waters of the business world, where competitors lurk and markets shift, the fortress of discretion stands as a beacon. Companies that prioritize trust and loyalty, bolstered by their walls of discretion, not only weather storms but thrive amidst them, setting course for success in both calm and turbulent seas.

Real World Business Examples of "The Fortress of Discretion: Building Trust and Loyalty":

- Apple's Commitment to Privacy: Apple has made privacy one of its core values, differentiating itself from competitors by promising discretion with user data. Their stance on refusing to unlock iPhones for third parties, even in high-profile cases with law enforcement, has solidified their reputation for discretion and has built trust with their consumer base.

- Costco's Employee Relations: Costco is known for treating its employees well, offering above-average wages, benefits, and job security. This approach has resulted in a loyal workforce with low turnover rates. By honoring its commitment to its employees, Costco has fostered trust and loyalty. (Smedra, 2022)

- Johnson & Johnson's Tylenol Recall (1982): When cyanide-laced Tylenol capsules led to several deaths, Johnson & Johnson quickly responded by recalling 31 million bottles of Tylenol, costing them over $100 million. Their swift and transparent action ensured consumer safety first, building trust and solidifying their reputation for responsible business practices. (NY Times, 2002)

Historical Pirate Examples of "The Fortress of Discretion: Building Trust and Loyalty":

- Blackbeard's Blockade of Charleston: In 1718, the infamous pirate Blackbeard blockaded Charleston's port, holding several hostages. Instead of harming them, he treated them well and released them once his demands (mostly for medical supplies) were met. This act might've spread stories about his relative discretion and fairness when dealing with hostages, perhaps influencing future encounters.

- Captain Kidd and the Adventure Galley: Kidd was given the ship Adventure Galley with the condition that he would share the spoils of his piracy with his sponsors. Despite many provocations and opportunities to betray this trust, Kidd tried to (mostly) operate within the bounds of his privateering mandate. This was his attempt to keep trust with his patrons, though he was later framed and met an unfortunate end.

- The Pirate Codes: Many pirate crews operated under a "pirate code" or set of articles which outlined the behavior expected on the ship, including how loot was divided and how disagreements were resolved. This was a way to build trust among a crew of outlaws, ensuring everyone knew what was expected and what they could expect in return.

Building and maintaining trust, both in the cutthroat world of piracy and in modern business, is critical for long-term success. The ability to foster loyalty, maintain discretion, and keep one's word can make or break reputations, relationships, and ventures.

Ah, my dear readers, as we draw the curtains on this chapter, it's essential to take a moment and truly absorb the weight of discretion in the vast seas of business. Just as the vast oceans are deep and mysterious, so too are the intricate workings of the corporate world. The parallels between the cunning pirates of yore and today's astute business leaders are striking. Both understand the immense value of what's hidden, of what's left unsaid, and the power that such secrecy wields.

In the world of pirates, the code "Dead Men Tell No Tales" wasn't just a warning; it was a philosophy. It was an understanding that the secrets of the seas, once revealed, could lead to one's undoing. It was a constant reminder that in a world filled with treachery and deceit, silence was often the best weapon. Today, in our hyper-connected world, where information can be disseminated globally in mere seconds, the essence of this philosophy is more relevant than ever. Companies are constantly under the microscope, scrutinized by competitors, regulators, and the public at large. In such an environment, the ability to guard one's secrets, to exercise discretion, becomes a superpower.

But discretion isn't just about keeping secrets; it's about building trust. It's about signaling to your stakeholders - be it employees, partners, or customers - that you value and respect the sanctity of information. It's about creating an environment where people feel safe to share, innovate, and collaborate, knowing that their contributions will be protected. This trust, once established, becomes the bedrock of loyalty, commitment, and long-term success.

So, as we set sail from this chapter, let the winds of discretion fill your sails. Let the tales of pirates, with their codes and cunning, inspire you to navigate the choppy waters of business with wisdom and integrity. Remember, in the grand game of business, as in the high seas, sometimes what you don't reveal is just as important as what you do. Guard your treasures, trust wisely, and always remember the words of Captain Martin Marlinspike: "In the vast oceans of commerce, silence isn't just golden; it's the very key to survival and success." Until our next adventure, may your compass always point true, and may discretion be your guiding star.

Chapter 7: "A Pirate's Treasure Isn't Always Gold" - Valuing Intangibles in the Corporate World

Ahoy, my astute navigators of the corporate seas and daring office-bound buccaneers! Prepare to set sail on a chapter that unveils the hidden treasures lying beneath the surface—treasures that, much like the secrets whispered by the wind, are intangible but invaluable. As we delve into the stories of pirates and the tapestry of modern business, we'll discover that not all riches can be measured in gold and gems. I, Captain Martin Marlinspike, shall be your guide as we navigate the uncharted waters of valuing intangibles in the ever-evolving corporate realm.

Imagine the pirates of yore, their eyes aflame with visions of glittering treasures. Yet, beyond the glistening loot, they held an understanding that some treasures were beyond measure—loyal crews who'd follow them to the ends of the earth, a reputation that struck fear into the hearts of enemies, and alliances that brought strength in unity. Similarly, today's business arena is a bustling bazaar of not just tangibles but also the intangibles that breathe life into an organization's essence.

In this chapter, the map unfurls to reveal these intangible assets, guiding us through the uncharted territory where reputation, trust, and culture reign supreme. The legendary pirates who knew that their reputation could be more powerful than their cutlass, and the modern corporate giants that understand that a positive company culture can be a compass steering them to success, converge in this exploration. As we set sail, let us fathom the depths of these intangible treasures, drawing inspiration from the annals of history and weaving them into the fabric of modern business strategies. In the boundless expanse of the business world, it's often the currents unseen that chart the course of a journey, and so we embark on this voyage of discovery with eager hearts and curious minds

1. The Intangible Gold: Brand Reputation

For pirates, reputation wasn't just a word; it was a weapon. A fearsome reputation could make entire fleets tremble and towns surrender without a single cannonball fired. In the corporate realm, brand reputation holds a similar power. It's an intangible asset, but its value is immeasurable. A company with a solid reputation finds it easier to launch new products, enter new markets, and command premium prices. It's not just about what you sell; it's about how the world perceives you. A strong brand reputation acts as a shield against negative publicity and a magnet for opportunities. It's the culmination of years of consistent quality, customer service, and public perception. In the age of social media, where news travels at the speed of light, maintaining a pristine reputation is both a challenge and a necessity.

- **Legacy and Longevity:** Just as pirate legends lived on for centuries, so do iconic brands. Companies like Coca-Cola, Rolex, and Apple have spent decades building their reputation, ensuring that their name is synonymous with quality and reliability. This legacy, in turn, guarantees a level of consumer trust and loyalty that new entrants might find challenging to replicate.

- **Influence and Impact:** Pirates often became influential figures, not just because of their plunder but because of their reputation. Similarly, companies with a strong reputation can influence market trends, set industry standards, and even sway public opinion. Their word becomes gold, and their endorsements can turn the tide for smaller brands and causes.

- **Recruitment and Retention:** Just as sailors would flock to join the crew of a legendary pirate, top talent gravitates towards companies with an outstanding reputation. A great brand reputation isn't just about attracting customers; it's about attracting the best human resources. Employees take pride in being associated with a respected brand, leading to higher job satisfaction and retention rates.

- **Crisis Management:** A well-established reputation can act as a buffer during times of crisis. Just as a pirate with a storied past might be given the benefit of the doubt by his crew during challenging times, consumers and stakeholders are more forgiving of missteps by brands with a track record of reliability and integrity.

- **Stakeholder Trust:** Reputation is not just about consumers. Stakeholders, including investors, suppliers, and partners, place immense value on a company's reputation. A respected brand often finds it easier to forge partnerships, secure investments, and negotiate favorable terms with suppliers.

- **Community and Connection:** Pirates built communities based on shared tales, mutual respect, and their collective reputation. Brands today foster communities of loyal followers who connect over shared values, experiences, and stories. This community doesn't just buy products; they become brand ambassadors, ensuring the company's reputation continues to grow organically.

In essence, while the tangible assets of a company can be measured in terms of numbers, the intangible gold of brand reputation is invaluable. Just as pirates nurtured their legends and tales, companies today must diligently cultivate, protect, and enhance their reputation in an ever-evolving marketplace.

Real World Business Examples of "The Intangible Gold: Brand Reputation":

- Coca-Cola: One of the most iconic brands globally, Coca-Cola's reputation has been built over more than a century. Their brand is synonymous with soft drinks, and their consistent marketing, community involvement, and global reach have made them a household name. Even when faced with challenges, such as the "New Coke" fiasco in the 1980s, the strength of their brand reputation helped them recover and remain a dominant force in the market. (coca-cola, n.d.)

- Toyota: Despite facing massive recalls in the late 2000s due to safety concerns, Toyota's long-standing reputation for reliability and quality helped the company weather the crisis. Their prompt response to the issues and commitment to quality reassured customers and maintained their position as one of the top automotive brands in the world. (Shih, 2022)

- Patagonia: This outdoor clothing and gear brand has built a reputation not just for quality products but also for its commitment to environmental sustainability and ethical practices. Their mission-driven approach has garnered a loyal customer base that aligns with the company's values, demonstrating the power of brand reputation in driving both sales and loyalty. (Wolfe, 2023)

Historical Pirate Examples of "The Intangible Gold: Brand Reputation":

- Blackbeard (Edward Teach): Blackbeard was as much a master of theatrics as he was a pirate. He would light fuses in his beard, creating an intimidating aura of smoke and flames around his head during battles. While he was undoubtedly a fearsome pirate, many of the tales about his cruelty were exaggerated or entirely false. His fearsome reputation ensured that many would surrender without a fight, saving both resources and lives.

- Bartholomew "Black Bart" Roberts: One of the most successful pirates of his time, Roberts captured over 400 ships during his career. His reputation was so formidable that many merchant ships would surrender immediately upon seeing his flag. While he was known for his strict discipline and adherence to his pirate code, his reputation made him one of the most feared pirates on the seas.

- Anne Bonny and Mary Read: These two female pirates challenged the gender norms of their time and built formidable reputations in the process. Their daring exploits were legendary, and they were known to be as fierce and ruthless as any male pirate. Their reputation alone was enough to make many adversaries think twice about engaging them.

In both the worlds of piracy and business, reputation is a powerful tool. It can open doors, deter adversaries, and create opportunities that might otherwise remain out of reach. Building and maintaining this reputation requires consistency, authenticity, and a commitment to one's values.

2. Loyalty: The Anchor of Success

In the unpredictable world of piracy, where mutinies were common and alliances fleeting, a pirate captain's most treasured asset was the loyalty of his crew. A loyal crew would follow their captain to the ends of the earth, through storms and battles. In the corporate landscape, loyalty, both of employees and customers, plays a similar pivotal role. Loyal employees drive innovation, ensure customer satisfaction, and become brand ambassadors. They're the backbone of a company, ensuring its smooth functioning and growth. On the other hand, loyal customers provide consistent revenue, free word-of-mouth marketing, and valuable feedback. They're the lifeblood of a business, ensuring its sustainability and success.

Real World Business Examples of "Loyalty: The Anchor of Success":

- Apple: Apple's customer base is famously loyal. Many Apple product users continue to buy Apple products and are highly resistant to switching to competing brands. This brand loyalty has been cultivated over years through innovative products, a consistent user experience, and a strong brand community.

- Southwest Airlines: In the airline industry, Southwest Airlines stands out for its strong employee loyalty. The company's unique corporate culture, which emphasizes employee empowerment and values, has led to a highly motivated workforce. This employee loyalty translates into high customer satisfaction, as loyal employees often go the extra mile for customers.

- Costco: The membership-based warehouse club has cultivated an impressive level of loyalty among both its employees and its customers. By providing employees with above-average wages and benefits, Costco ensures low turnover and high job satisfaction. Customers, in turn, are loyal due to the company's focus on high-quality products at competitive prices and exemplary customer service. (Smedra, 2022)

Historical Pirate Examples of "Loyalty: The Anchor of Success":

- Captain William Kidd: Initially a privateer, Kidd's loyalty to his home country of England was unquestionable. However, after being branded a pirate by the English, he believed he had evidence that would clear his name. His loyalty to his crew was also notable, as he tried to ensure they were treated fairly and equitably.

- Calico Jack Rackham: Known for his distinctive Jolly Roger flag and his partnership with female pirates Anne Bonny and Mary Read, Calico Jack had a loyal crew that stuck with him through various adventures. This loyalty was partly due to his democratic way of handling spoils and decisions, which was a trait common in many successful pirate crews.

- Bartholomew "Black Bart" Roberts: As previously mentioned, Roberts was one of the most successful pirates of his era. One of the keys to his success was the loyalty of his crew. Roberts was known to be a strict disciplinarian but was also fair, ensuring that the spoils of their raids were divided equitably among the crew. His leadership and sense of justice cultivated a strong sense of loyalty among his crew members.

In both the high seas and the corporate boardrooms, loyalty acts as a stabilizing force. It provides direction in uncertain times, fosters a sense of community and purpose, and ensures long-term success. Cultivating and maintaining loyalty requires trust, fairness, and a shared vision for the future.

3. Trust: The North Star of Business

In the treacherous world of piracy, where betrayal was common and alliances were often broken, trust was a rare and valuable commodity. It was the North Star, guiding pirates through challenges and ensuring lasting alliances. In the world of business, trust plays a similar guiding role. Whether it's trust between business partners, between a company and its customers, or between employers and employees, trust is the foundation of long-term success. It's the glue that holds partnerships together, the magnet that attracts customers, and the bond that ensures employee loyalty. In an era where consumers are bombarded with choices, trust is the intangible asset that can set a company apart.

- **Consumer Confidence:** Just as pirates had to trust their maps and compasses to lead them to treasure, consumers rely on brands that have earned their trust. Once established, this trust can lead to increased brand loyalty, word-of-mouth referrals, and a higher likelihood of consumers sticking with the brand even when competitors offer similar products at cheaper prices.

- **Stability in Partnerships:** In the volatile world of piracy, if two captains trusted each other, their crews could operate as a cohesive unit, increasing their chances of success. In business, when companies trust their partners, they can collaborate more effectively, share resources, and co-innovate, leading to products and services that can redefine markets.

- **Employee Morale and Productivity:** Just as a pirate crew's trust in their captain ensured smoother sailing and more effective combat, employees who trust their leadership are more engaged, motivated, and productive. They're more likely to go the extra mile, believe in the company's vision, and stay committed during challenging times.

- **Risk Management:** Trust acts as a buffer against uncertainties. In the unpredictable seas, pirates who trusted each other had better chances of navigating storms together. Similarly, in business, having a foundation of trust can help companies weather market fluctuations, regulatory changes, and unforeseen crises. Trusted brands often recover faster from negative publicity or product mishaps.

- **Investor Relations:** Just as pirate legends built on trust attracted more sailors to their cause, companies with a reputation for trustworthiness and transparency attract more investors. Trust assures stakeholders that the company will act with integrity, even when no one is watching.

- **Innovation and Growth:** Trust fosters an environment where ideas are shared freely. In a trusted workspace, employees are more likely to share innovative ideas, collaborate on projects, and believe in the company's direction. This atmosphere can be a hotbed for innovation, much like how trust among pirate allies could lead to more successful raids and discoveries.

- **Building Communities:** Trusted brands have the power to create communities around them. These communities, be it of loyal customers, supportive stakeholders, or dedicated employees, act as amplifiers, echoing the brand's virtues and bringing in more people into their fold.

In the vast and complex sea of business, where competition is fierce and the landscape ever-changing, trust is the constant star that companies can navigate by. It's not just about making a sale or sealing a deal; it's about building relationships that stand the test of time. Just as pirates valued trust above gold, for businesses, trust is the treasure that ensures enduring success.

Real World Business Examples of "Trust: The North Star of Business":

- Amazon: Founded by Jeff Bezos, Amazon built its massive customer base on trust. From its early days as an online bookstore, its commitment to customer service, reliable delivery, and easy returns made consumers trust Amazon for their online purchases. This trust enabled Amazon to expand into numerous other product categories and services. (DePillis & Sherman, 2018)

- Toyota: In the automotive world, Toyota has long held a reputation for reliability. When a series of recalls threatened this reputation in the late 2000s, Toyota undertook a massive effort to address the issues and rebuild consumer trust. Their commitment to quality and swift response to problems has helped maintain their reputation for reliability. (Shih, 2022)

- Airbnb: When Airbnb was first conceived, the idea of staying in a stranger's home or letting strangers stay in your home was novel and required a leap of faith. Airbnb built trust through a robust review system, transparent host-guest communication, and guarantees against property damage, thus fostering trust in the sharing economy.

Historical Pirate Examples of "Trust: The North Star of Business":

- Blackbeard (Edward Teach): While Blackbeard cultivated a fearsome reputation, he often used intimidation over violence, and many accounts suggest he was a shrewd leader who understood the importance of trust among his crew. His partnership with such pirates as Stede Bonnet indicates that Blackbeard was capable of forming alliances based on mutual trust.

- Captain Henry Morgan: Morgan's ability to rally pirates and buccaneers for his raids, especially the famous attack on Panama, was based on his reputation and the trust his men had in him. They believed in his leadership and trusted that following him would lead to substantial booty.

- Ching Shih: After the death of her pirate husband, Ching took over his fleet and established a strict code of conduct for her pirates, which included provisions against rape and the fair distribution of booty. Her leadership, based on trust and discipline, made her one of the most powerful and successful pirates in history, commanding a fleet of hundreds of ships. (Banerji, 2022)

In both piracy and business, trust acts as a guiding principle, ensuring cohesive operations, strategic partnerships, and lasting relationships. Building and maintaining this trust requires consistent actions, transparency, and mutual respect.

4. Innovation: The Wind in the Sails

Pirates, often seen as mere plunderers, were in fact innovators. They developed new navigation techniques, improved ship designs, and even devised early forms of democracy. In the corporate world, innovation is the wind that propels a company forward. It's the force that drives growth, opens new revenue streams, and keeps competitors at bay. In the ever-evolving market landscape, companies that fail to innovate are often left behind, while those that embrace innovation set the course for others to follow.

- **Evolution of Tactics:** Much like how pirates often altered their strategies, changing their tactics to deal with more fortified towns or stronger naval presences, businesses too must evolve their methods. In the face of evolving consumer needs or industry disruptions, innovative strategies can distinguish a leader from a follower.

- **Embracing Technology:** Pirates were among the first to embrace emerging nautical technologies of their time, giving them an edge in their endeavors. Similarly, businesses today have the digital realm, with AI, machine learning, and big data analytics providing avenues for innovation, enhancing customer experiences, streamlining operations, and unlocking new potentials.

- **Fostering a Culture of Innovation:** It wasn't just the pirate captains who came up with strategies; crews often had a say, thanks to their early democratic systems. In modern businesses, encouraging a culture where every team member feels empowered to suggest improvements or new ideas can be the key to unlocking groundbreaking innovations.

- **Anticipating Trends:** Pirates had an uncanny ability to predict trade routes and the movement of merchant ships, which made their raids successful. In business, being able to anticipate market trends or shifts in consumer behavior ensures that companies can tailor their innovations to what the market will want next.

- **Diversification:** Just as pirates wouldn't rely on raiding a single type of ship or a single trade route, businesses must diversify their innovative efforts. This could be in the form of expanding product lines, exploring different market segments, or even venturing into different industries altogether.

- **Collaborative Innovations:** Alliances among pirate crews led to sharing of knowledge and resources, enabling them to take on larger targets. Similarly, in the business world, partnerships, joint ventures, and even open-source collaborations can drive innovation, pooling together expertise and resources to achieve common goals.

- **Adapting to Failures:** Not every pirate raid was successful. However, they learned from their failures and adapted. In the realm of business, not every innovation will be a hit. But it's essential to learn from these misses, iterate, and come back with improved offerings.

- **Sustainability:** Pirates had to ensure the sustainability of their operations, ensuring they didn't deplete an area of all its resources. Modern businesses too must innovate with sustainability in mind, ensuring that they meet present needs without compromising the ability of future generations to meet their own.

Innovation, be it on the high seas or in the boardroom, is about thinking differently, taking calculated risks, and not being afraid to challenge the status quo. It's the wind that not only propels the ship forward but ensures it remains agile, efficient, and ahead of the curve in its journey.

Real World Business Examples of "Innovation: The Wind in the Sails":

- Spotify: Instead of purchasing albums or individual songs, Spotify offered a subscription model that allowed users to stream music. This innovation disrupted the music industry, providing artists a platform to reach audiences directly and giving users access to a vast library of music at their fingertips. (Griffith, 2018)

- Square: Jack Dorsey's Square revolutionized the payment industry, especially for small businesses. Before Square, many small businesses struggled with expensive and complicated point-of-sale systems. Square introduced a simple card reader that attached to smartphones, allowing even the smallest businesses to accept card payments easily. (Smith, 2020)

- Beyond Meat: The company innovated in the food sector by developing plant-based meat alternatives that closely resemble the taste and texture of real meat. This innovation is not just about catering to vegetarians but is seen as a sustainable solution to the environmental issues caused by traditional meat production. (Garza, 2023)

Historical Pirate Examples of "Innovation: The Wind in the Sails":

- William Dampier: Before turning pirate, Dampier was an English explorer and navigator. He was the first Englishman to explore parts of Australia and the first to circumnavigate the world three times. His detailed logs and maps, including wind and ocean currents, were instrumental in helping future navigators and pirates. (Princeton.edu, n.d.)

- Bartholomew Roberts (Black Bart): While Roberts was known for his capture count, he was also notable for his innovative tactics. He was known to fly deceptive flags to get close to his prey, only raising the pirate flag when it was too late for the victim to escape. This tactic was adopted by many pirates after him.

- Henry Every (or Avery): Every led one of the most profitable pirate raids in history against the Mughal ship Ganj-i-Sawai. The innovation here was in the target: Instead of attacking smaller merchant ships as most pirates did, Every and his crew took on one of the largest ships in the world and succeeded, resulting in riches beyond most pirates' wildest dreams.

- Anne Bonny and Mary Read: These two female pirates defied the gender norms of their time. In an era where the seas were dominated by men, they not only disguised themselves as men to be part of pirate crews but also redefined their roles, innovating their way in the male-dominated world of piracy.

For both pirates and businesses, innovation is the key to exploring new horizons, overcoming challenges, and staying ahead of the curve.

As our voyage through this chapter draws to a close, let's anchor our thoughts and reflect on the intangible treasures that truly matter. In the grand tapestry of business, it's often the unseen threads that hold everything together. Just as pirates, with their keen eyes, could spot a distant ship or a hidden cove, businesses must develop the vision to recognize and nurture their intangible assets. These assets, be it reputation, loyalty, trust, or innovation, are the true treasures that can set a company apart in the crowded marketplace.

In the corporate seas, where storms of competition and waves of change are ever-present, it's these intangible assets that act as the lighthouse, guiding a company to safe harbors of success. They shape perceptions, foster loyalty, drive innovation, and create a legacy. They're the unseen forces that propel a company forward, ensuring its growth, sustainability, and success.

So, as you chart your course in the corporate world, remember to value these intangible treasures. For they, much like the loyalty of a pirate crew or the reputation of a fearsome captain, can be the difference between success and failure. And as Captain Martin Marlinspike would say, "In the grand adventure of business, it's not the tangible gold that counts, but the intangible treasures that truly matter." So, set your sights on these treasures, value them, nurture them, and let them guide you to unparalleled success. Until our next adventure, may your compass always point to true north, and may your journey be filled with success, adventure, and a touch of pirate flair. Fair winds and following seas.

Chapter 8: "Take What You Can, Give Nothing Back" - The Delicate Balance of Leadership and Entrepreneurship in Business

Aaaarrrrgggghhhh!, seekers of strategic wisdom! As we navigate the uncharted waters of business, guided by the tales of daring pirates, we set our course towards the heart of leadership and entrepreneurship. I am Captain Martin Marlinspike, your dedicated helmswoman on this enlightening voyage, and I've witnessed the ebb and flow of leadership both on the high seas and within the bustling world of commerce. The world of piracy, with its legends of audacious raids, hidden treasures, and cunning captains, offers a treasure trove of lessons for today's leaders and aspiring entrepreneurs. Beyond the surface of swashbuckling escapades, the pirates of old were masters of strategic leadership, possessing insights that remain as relevant today as they were during the golden age of piracy.

In the tumultuous realm of piracy, where the seas were teeming with rival crews, naval forces, and hidden dangers, strategic leadership was not a luxury; it was a necessity for survival. Pirate captains, often operating as charismatic leaders of diverse crews, had to navigate treacherous waters, make split-second decisions, and inspire loyalty among their crew members. The phrase "Take What You Can, Give Nothing Back" symbolized their pragmatic approach to seizing opportunities and maximizing gains. They understood that leadership wasn't just about commanding authority but also about making calculated choices that benefited the crew's objectives and their own legacy.

Now, you might wonder how the codes of pirates, with their ruthless pursuit of riches, apply to the world of ethical leadership and entrepreneurship. The answer lies in the principles that underpin their actions. While the pirates' approach may seem cutthroat, it's the underlying strategy that holds the key. In today's fast-paced business landscape, effective leaders and entrepreneurs must be adept at seizing opportunities, making tough decisions, and strategically allocating resources. The most successful ventures are those that recognize the value of innovation, risk-taking, and the pursuit of strategic advantage.

As we delve into this chapter, let us draw inspiration from the pirates of old. Let us explore the multifaceted world of strategic leadership, where audacity is tempered by calculated risk, and where the pursuit of gain aligns with a broader vision. Together, we shall uncover the art of seizing opportunities, making strategic choices, and cultivating a leadership style that fosters growth and innovation. Join me, dear reader, as we set sail on this voyage, navigating the uncharted waters of strategic leadership and entrepreneurship, guided by the timeless wisdom of pirates.

1. Seizing Opportunities: The Art of Taking

Aaaarrrrgggghhhh!, my intrepid navigators of the corporate seas! Captain Martin Marlinspike here, ready to embark on yet another thrilling voyage into the depths of business wisdom. Today, we set our sights on a pirate adage that's as cunning as it is controversial: "Take what you can, give nothing back." At first glance, it might seem like a ruthless mantra, advocating for selfishness and greed. But, as with all things pirate, there's more beneath the surface. This chapter will dive into the nuanced interpretation of this saying, exploring its relevance and application in the realms of leadership and entrepreneurship.

In the unpredictable waters of business, leaders and entrepreneurs often find themselves in situations where they must seize opportunities and make the most of them. But how does one balance ambition with ethics? How does one take without becoming a taker? And how does one ensure that in the pursuit of success, they don't leave a trail of destruction in their wake? Join me, dear reader, as we navigate these questions and uncover the true essence of this pirate wisdom.

- **An Opportunity on the Horizon:** Every pirate worth their salt can recall the thrill of spotting a ship on the horizon, laden with treasures. The sight sparked an internal battle: to chase or to retreat? In the business world, these ships represent opportunities — be it a new market, a potential partnership, or an innovative product idea. Spotting them is only the first step; the real challenge lies in assessing their value and deciding whether or not to seize them.

- **The Calculated Risk:** Pirates, contrary to popular depictions, weren't always reckless. They weighed the potential rewards against the risks. Similarly, successful entrepreneurs understand that not every opportunity is worth chasing. They employ research, intuition, and foresight, ensuring they don't spread their resources too thin or venture into stormy waters unprepared.

- **The Ethical Compass:** "Take what you can" doesn't grant a free pass to trample on others. Ethical considerations are paramount. The most revered pirates had codes of conduct, which while flexible, were never abandoned. Modern businesses too should have their ethical guidelines. Taking an opportunity should never come at the undue expense of others.

- **Generosity in Leadership:** "Give nothing back" is not an endorsement of stinginess. In the pirate context, it referred more to not showing vulnerability to adversaries. In business, it can mean retaining one's competitive edge. However, within a company, a leader should be generous — with praise, with rewards, and with opportunities for their team.

- **Sustainability in Seizing:** The tales of pirates burying their treasures are legendary. They understood the value of saving for the future. Similarly, when seizing opportunities, businesses should think long-term. Quick profits can be enticing, but sustainable growth ensures the ship sails smoothly for years to come.

- **Navigating the Gray Areas:** The waters are never just black or white; there's a vast gray expanse where most decisions lie. Entrepreneurs often have to navigate these murky waters, deciding how aggressively to pursue an opportunity or when to hold back. The pirate code serves as a reminder to be agile, adaptive, and always alert.

Seizing opportunities, like the art of piracy, requires a blend of courage, cunning, and compassion. It's about recognizing the potential for growth, assessing the environment, and making informed decisions. But more than anything, it's about ensuring that in the quest for treasures, we don't lose sight of our moral compass. So, as we set sail on this entrepreneurial journey, head the advice of ole' Captain Marlinspike and strive to master the art of taking, without losing your soul.

Real World Business Examples of "Seizing Opportunities: The Art of Taking":

- Uber: When Travis Kalanick and Garrett Camp first envisioned a ride-sharing platform, traditional taxi services dominated urban transportation. But they saw a gap: many cities had unreliable taxi systems and rising smartphone penetration. Seizing this opportunity, they launched Uber, not just offering a service but revolutionizing urban transportation globally. (Blystone, 2023)

- Netflix: Originally a DVD-by-mail service, Reed Hastings and his team recognized the potential of streaming technology. Instead of sticking to their old model, they seized the opportunity to shift to streaming, eventually outpacing traditional cable services and changing how we consume media. (MISRA, 2020)

- Dollar Shave Club: When Michael Dubin started the company, big brands dominated the razor market. He seized the opportunity by offering a subscription model for quality razors at a fraction of the price. Using a unique marketing approach with a viral video, he disrupted the razor industry and eventually sold the company for a billion dollars to Unilever. (Sherry, 2022)

Historical Pirate Examples of "Seizing Opportunities: The Art of Taking":

- Sir Francis Drake: Commissioned by Queen Elizabeth I, Drake's voyages had two purposes: exploration and piracy. He saw the opportunity to seize Spanish treasure ships returning from the New World, enriching himself and the English treasury. His most famous victory came against the Spanish Silver Train at Nombre de Dios in Panama, where he managed to get away with a vast amount of treasure. (Britannica, n.d.)

- Black Bart (Bartholomew Roberts): Unlike many pirates who chose easy targets, Black Bart saw opportunities where others didn't. He captured ships off the coast of Africa and even took over entire fleets, seizing more than 400 ships during his career, making him one of the most successful pirates in history.

- Jean Lafitte: Recognizing the strategic importance of New Orleans and its surrounding waterways, Lafitte established a pirate kingdom in Barataria Bay, selling smuggled goods to local merchants. When the War of 1812 broke out, he seized the opportunity to offer his services and insider knowledge to General Andrew Jackson, playing a crucial role in the American victory at the Battle of New Orleans. (National Parks Service, 2020)

In both realms, the ability to identify, act upon, and capitalize on opportunities determines success. However, as our pirate adage hints, the key lies in taking without harming, ensuring that our actions benefit not just ourselves but the broader community or ecosystem.

2. Ethical Ambition: Taking Without Being a Taker

The pirate mantra might seem to advocate for unabashed greed, but in the intricate dance of business, it's not about mindlessly taking. It's about understanding one's worth and ensuring that you're adequately compensated for your efforts, skills, and risks. However, this ambition must be tempered with ethics. In a world where reputation is invaluable, leaders and entrepreneurs must ensure that their ambition doesn't trample on others. It's about negotiating fiercely but fairly, about claiming one's share without depriving others of theirs. This delicate balance between ambition and ethics is what distinguishes great leaders from mere opportunists. It's what ensures long-term success, fosters trust, and builds a legacy that goes beyond profits.

- **Ambition With a Heart:** At the core of ethical ambition is the idea that you can strive for success and greatness while maintaining a heart of empathy and consideration. Much like how pirates had their code, which, though non-traditional, still had rules to ensure some form of order, business leaders should adhere to a code that values human connections and respects boundaries.

- **Value-Driven Success:** A business or individual fueled by ethical ambition seeks to climb the ladder of success without pushing others down. They measure success not just in profits or accolades, but in the positive impact they make in their community, industry, and on their team.

- **Stakeholder Consideration:** Modern businesses don't operate in a vacuum. Leaders must consider the effects of their decisions on all stakeholders – from employees and shareholders to the environment and communities they operate in. Ethical ambition ensures that all stakeholders are considered and that decisions made benefit the broader ecosystem.

- **Authentic Relationships:** Building relationships based on mutual respect and understanding is at the heart of ethical ambition. It's about creating networks and partnerships where all parties feel valued and not just a means to an end.

- **The Power of Fair Play:** In a world where cutthroat competition is often glamorized, the ethos of ethical ambition champions the idea of fair play. It's about competing with integrity, ensuring that even in the heat of business battles, the rules of decency are never sidestepped.

- **Growth and Responsibility:** With growth comes increased responsibility. Ethical ambition understands this correlation and ensures that as businesses grow, they take on more significant roles in community building, social responsibility, and ensuring the well-being of all involved.

- **Long-Term Vision:** Whereas unchecked ambition might chase short-term gains, ethical ambition is always aligned with a long-term vision. It understands that real, lasting success isn't about quick wins but about building a sustainable legacy rooted in values.

- **The Ripple Effect:** One of the most profound impacts of ethical ambition is the ripple effect it creates. When one leader or business operates from this perspective, it sets a precedent, influencing others to adopt similar practices, thereby elevating the entire industry or community.

In essence, ethical ambition is about redefining the concept of taking. It's about understanding that true success isn't just about amassing wealth or power, but about doing so in a manner that uplifts others, contributes positively to the world, and leaves a legacy of integrity and respect. It's the compass that ensures that in the voyage of ambition, the ship stays on a course that honors both the journey and its travelers.

Real World Business Examples of "Ethical Ambition: Taking Without Being a Taker":

- Patagonia: This outdoor clothing company, under the leadership of Yvon Chouinard, has built its brand on the intersection of profit and environmental responsibility. While it takes its fair share of profits, it's committed to sustainable practices, donates a portion of its sales to environmental causes, and has even encouraged consumers to buy less of its product to reduce environmental impact. (Wolfe, 2023)

- The Body Shop: Founded by Anita Roddick, The Body Shop carved a niche in the cosmetics industry with a strong stand against animal testing and a commitment to fair trade. While the company pursued profits, it also focused on ethical sourcing of ingredients, ensuring that the communities that supplied them benefited fairly from their trade. (Entrepreneur.com, 2008)

- Ben & Jerry's: The ice cream brand, established by Ben Cohen and Jerry Greenfield, is a prime example of a business that seeks profit without compromising on its values. Apart from creating delectable flavors, the company is known for its social initiatives, equitable pay structures, and sourcing practices that prioritize both the environment and producers. (Fabry, 2018)

Historical Pirate Examples of "Ethical Ambition: Taking Without Being a Taker":

- Captain William Kidd: Before being notoriously known as a pirate, Kidd was actually a privateer who was supposed to hunt pirates and French ships. While he did seize ships and treasures, he always maintained that he operated under the permissions granted to him by his commission. His later trial and execution are still subjects of debate regarding its fairness.

- Samuel Bellamy: Known as "Black Sam," Bellamy was described by some as the "Robin Hood of the Sea." While he did plunder ships, he was also known for his democratic and generous nature. Captured crews spoke of his kindness, often giving them better ships than the ones he took from them.

- Captain Henry Avery: Dubbed "The Arch Pirate," Avery was renowned for his capture of the Mughal ship Ganj-i-Sawai. What's noteworthy is that despite the massive wealth he acquired, Avery was known for ensuring his crew received a fair share, unlike many pirate captains who took the lion's share for themselves.

These examples showcase that, while ambition is essential in both business and piracy, it must be accompanied by a moral compass. By ensuring that their pursuits didn't harm others, these figures were able to achieve success without compromising their ethics.

3. Giving Back: The Responsibility of Success

While the adage might suggest a one-sided approach, true leadership transcends this. In the realm of business, there's an inherent responsibility that comes with success. Leaders and entrepreneurs, as they climb the ladder of success, must ensure they're not leaving a void below. Giving back isn't just about philanthropy; it's about mentorship, creating opportunities for others, and fostering a culture of growth and inclusivity. It's about recognizing that true success isn't measured by what you accumulate, but by what you contribute. Whether it's imparting knowledge, investing in community projects, or supporting causes, giving back is what enriches a leader's journey and ensures that their path to success benefits more than just themselves.

Real World Business Examples of "Giving Back: The Responsibility of Success":

- Bill and Melinda Gates Foundation: Founded by Microsoft co-founder Bill Gates and his then-wife Melinda, this foundation is one of the largest private philanthropic organizations globally. With a mission to enhance healthcare and reduce extreme poverty globally, they have contributed billions to various causes, especially in the fields of health, education, and technology.

- Warren Buffett's Pledge: One of the world's most successful investors, Warren Buffett, has pledged to give away 99% of his wealth to philanthropic causes, mainly through the Bill and Melinda Gates Foundation. This significant commitment to giving back is a testament to his belief in the responsibility that comes with immense success. (Fortune, 2022)

- Salesforce's 1-1-1 Model: Under the leadership of Marc Benioff, Salesforce adopted a unique philanthropic model. The 1-1-1 model means they dedicate 1% of their product, 1% of their equity, and 1% of their employees' time to charitable causes. This integrated philanthropic approach has been replicated by many other companies, showcasing how businesses can embed giving back into their operational model. (Sheridan, 2010)

Historical Pirate Examples of "Giving Back: The Responsibility of Success":

- Captain Kidd's Investment: Before turning pirate, Captain William Kidd was a respected privateer. Kidd financed part of his voyages, and when he captured prizes, he ensured that some of the profits went back to his investors, which included notable members of the British aristocracy.

- Blackbeard's Blockade: Edward Teach, better known as Blackbeard, is one of history's most notorious pirates. However, there were instances where he used his influence for the good of the community. In one notable instance, Blackbeard blockaded the port of Charles Town (Charleston), not for personal riches, but to secure medical supplies for his crew and the local inhabitants.

- Bartholomew Roberts and 'The Pirate Code': While not philanthropy in the traditional sense, the infamous pirate Bartholomew Roberts is known to have enforced a Pirate Code amongst his crew. This code emphasized fairness, ensured that injured pirates received compensation, and that spoils were divided equitably among the crew. Such a code, rare in an era and profession known for treachery, showcased a form of 'giving back' to those who served under him.

Each of these examples, from both the business world and the high seas, showcases the diverse ways leaders have realized the importance of giving back and the responsibility that success bestows upon them.

As we drop anchor on this chapter's voyage, it's evident that the audacious strategies of pirates and the sophisticated tactics of modern-day business leaders aren't worlds apart. They share an undercurrent: the need for strategic leadership balanced with ethical considerations. Both realms demand an eye for opportunity, a hand steady enough to take but gentle enough to give, and a heart grounded in principles.

The pirate maxim, "Take What You Can, Give Nothing Back," is more than a call for opportunism. It's a nuanced strategy that resonates with the challenges faced by today's leaders and entrepreneurs. To truly succeed in the world of business, as in piracy, one must recognize when to seize, how to grow without harm, and the critical importance of giving back. This three-pronged approach ensures that ambition doesn't overshadow ethics, and success becomes more than just personal gain. It evolves into a legacy.

Much like the tales of legendary pirates, the stories of successful business leaders are passed down and revered, not just for their triumphs but for the impact they leave behind. The greatest leaders, whether on the high seas or in the towering skyscrapers of commerce, understand that leadership isn't about amassing treasures but enriching the lives of those they touch. As we set our compass for future endeavors, let us be inspired by these lessons from the depths of history, ensuring our pursuits benefit the world at large and leave behind a legacy worth celebrating. So, fellow traveler, as you steer your ship through the turbulent waters of business, remember to balance ambition with responsibility, ensuring your voyage benefits not just you but all those you encounter along the way. Sail on, with purpose and principle, and may your leadership journey be as legendary as those of the pirates of old.

Chapter 9: "Even Pirates, Before They Attack Another Ship, Hoist a Black Flag" - Signaling Intent in the Corporate Seas

Ahoy, my corporate darlings and desk-bound adventurers! It's Captain Martin Marlinspike, with a swish of my skirt and a twinkle in my eye, here to sprinkle a touch of sassy pirate wisdom onto the often too-serious world of business. The black flag wasn't just a pirate's accessory—it was a bold statement, much like a woman's favorite red lipstick. In today's corporate landscape, if you're not broadcasting your intentions, honey, you're just another ship lost at sea. This chapter will delve deep into the importance of clear communication, setting expectations, and the dangers of ambiguity, drawing parallels from the world of pirates. Just as the black flag was a symbol of imminent action, so too must businesses signal their intentions to navigate the turbulent waters of the market. In a world filled with noise and distractions, having a clear and distinct message can be the difference between being noticed and being overlooked. The importance of signaling intent, much like the pirates of old, is paramount in ensuring that your business sails smoothly, avoiding the treacherous waters of miscommunication and ambiguity.

1. The Symbolism of the Black Flag: Clear Communication

When a black flag was hoisted atop a ship's mast, it sent a clear message to all who saw it: pirates were near, and they meant business. This clarity of intent, this unmistakable signal, is something that's sorely needed in the corporate world. In a landscape filled with noise, competition, and ever-shifting market dynamics, clear communication becomes the beacon that guides a company forward. It ensures that everyone, from stakeholders to employees, understands the company's direction, goals, and strategies. Without this clarity, confusion can reign, leading to inefficiencies, misaligned teams, and missed market opportunities. In essence, just as the black flag was an unmistakable symbol of a pirate ship's intent, so too must businesses have clear and unmistakable communication to signal their intent in the market. In the vast sea of information, only those with a clear message can hope to stand out and make an impact. A company's vision, mission, and values should be as clear as the black flag on a pirate ship, signaling its intent and direction to all who encounter it.

Real World Business Examples of "The Symbolism of the Black Flag: Clear Communication":

Apple's "Think Different" Campaign: Apple has always been known for its clarity of vision and design ethos. When they launched their "Think Different" campaign in the late 1990s, it wasn't just about promoting their products. It was a clear declaration of Apple's intent to challenge the status quo and redefine technology's role in our lives. The campaign, through its iconic images and succinct message, communicated

- Apple's brand philosophy with unmatched clarity. (Mupeti, 2023)

- Nike's "Just Do It" Slogan: Nike's famous three-word slogan is a masterclass in clear communication. Within those three words, Nike encapsulated its brand's essence, its ethos of perseverance, and its encouragement to individuals to transcend their limits. By keeping it simple and direct, Nike managed to communicate its brand promise to millions globally. (Restrepo, 2022)

- Southwest Airlines' "Transfarency" Initiative: In an industry notorious for hidden fees, Southwest Airlines introduced its "Transfarency" campaign. This initiative was a pledge that the price you see is the price you pay, with no hidden fees attached. By coining a new term and launching a campaign around it, Southwest clearly communicated its commitment to transparent pricing, setting itself apart from competitors. (Southwest Airlines, 2015)

Historical Pirate Examples of "The Symbolism of the Black Flag: Clear Communication":

- Blackbeard's Own Flag: Edward Teach, known as Blackbeard, had a flag that was particularly terrifying. It showcased a horned skeleton holding an hourglass in one hand, signifying that time was running out, and a spear pointing to a heart on the other side. This clearly communicated his ruthlessness and the dire fate awaiting those who opposed him.

- Calico Jack's Flag: The pirate Calico Jack, known for his association with the female pirates Anne Bonny and Mary Read, had a distinct flag that showed a skull with two crossed cutlasses beneath it. This was a clear symbol of the threat of violence that awaited those who resisted his crew's advances.

- Black Bart's Flag: Bartholomew Roberts, or Black Bart, was one of the most successful pirates of his time. His flag depicted a figure standing on two skulls, labeled "ABH" and "AMH," representing the heads of a Barbadian and a Martiniquian, respectively. This was a clear message to his enemies, especially those from Barbados and Martinique, about his intentions and his disdain for them.

In both realms, the importance of clear, unmistakable communication is evident. While the mediums and methods might differ, the core principle remains: sending a direct, unmistakable message to one's audience ensures alignment, understanding, and a strong brand or identity presence.

2. Team Building: Setting Expectations and Boundaries

Every successful pirate crew operated under a set of rules or a code. This wasn't just about sharing loot or deciding punishments; it was about ensuring every crew member knew their role and what was expected of them. In the corporate world, setting clear expectations is equally crucial. It provides a framework within which employees can operate, fostering a sense of trust, accountability, and cohesion. When everyone knows their role, boundaries, and the expectations set upon them, the entire team functions more efficiently. It reduces friction, minimizes misunderstandings, and ensures that everyone is pulling in the same direction.

Much like a pirate crew under a black flag, a corporate team with clear expectations and boundaries is a force to be reckoned with. A well-informed team is a motivated team, and a motivated team can achieve wonders. Clear expectations also ensure that there's a shared vision, and when everyone is aligned with this vision, the company can move forward cohesively, much like a well-oiled ship.

Real World Business Examples of "Team Building: Setting Expectations and Boundaries":

- Google's Project Aristotle: In a bid to understand the secrets of successful teams, Google embarked on a two-year study called Project Aristotle. The primary discovery was that the most successful teams fostered psychological safety. This is an environment where team members feel safe taking risks, knowing they won't face punishment or humiliation. By setting clear expectations around communication, respect, and feedback, Google teams could build a foundation of trust, ensuring everyone knew their role and boundaries. (Burnison, 2019)

- Netflix's Culture Deck: In 2009, Netflix released its culture deck, a 127-slide presentation that laid out the company's philosophy, including its emphasis on freedom and responsibility. Rather than micromanaging its employees with endless rules, Netflix set clear expectations about performance and accountability, granting employees the freedom to innovate within those boundaries. This culture of high performance and clear expectations has been credited as one of the key drivers behind Netflix's success. (McCord, 2014)

- Zappos' Core Values: Zappos, the online shoe retailer, has a set of 10 core values that guide everything from hiring decisions to daily operations. These values include delivering "WOW" service, being humble, and pursuing growth and learning. By setting these clear expectations and boundaries, Zappos ensures its teams remain aligned with the company's overarching vision and mission. (Frampton, 2020)

Historical Pirate Examples of "Team Building: Setting Expectations and Boundaries":

- The Pirate Code of Bartholomew Roberts: Black Bart's code was one of the most well-known among pirates. It had articles that dictated everything from the distribution of loot to consequences for abandoning one's post during battle. This code ensured that each member of his crew knew exactly

what was expected of them and the repercussions for any
breaches.

- The Articles of Captain John Phillips: Captain Phillips' code
  was a set of articles that governed everything from gambling
  onboard (which was prohibited) to compensation for injuries
  sustained during their endeavors. By clearly outlining these
  rules, Captain Phillips set clear expectations for his crew's
  behavior.

- The Chasse-Partie Agreement: This was a type of contract
  used mainly by French privateers, and it detailed the
  distribution of the spoils after a successful raid. It served as an
  agreement between the captain and the crew, ensuring that
  everyone knew their share and minimized conflicts related to
  loot distribution. (Milligan, 2022)

Both in the tumultuous world of pirates and the corporate landscape,
setting expectations and establishing boundaries have been pivotal
for ensuring success. It's the framework that guides actions, fosters
trust, and ensures that each member knows their place and purpose
within the larger group.

3. Interpersonal Communication: Signaling Intent

In the world of pirates, the black flag was more than just a symbol; it
was a statement of intent. It told everyone exactly what the pirates
were about to do. Similarly, in the corporate world, signaling intent in
interpersonal communication is of paramount importance. It ensures
that everyone is on the same page, reducing the chances of
misunderstandings or misinterpretations. Effective communication
fosters a culture of transparency and trust, where employees feel
valued and informed. In an environment where information flows
freely and intent is clearly signaled, teams can collaborate more

effectively, projects are more likely to succeed, and the overall morale of the organization remains high. It's not just about conveying information; it's about ensuring that the information is understood, absorbed, and acted upon. This clear signaling of intent in communication can be the difference between a project's success and failure, between a motivated team and a disengaged one.

Real World Business Examples of "Interpersonal Communication: Signaling Intent":

- Product Launch Announcement: When a tech company is about to launch a new product, they use various channels to signal their intent. They might send out press releases, host preview events, and update their website with teaser content. This clear and coordinated communication signals their intent to the market, generating buzz and anticipation among customers and investors alike. This was evident when Apple announced the launch of the iPhone. Months before the actual release, they provided glimpses of the features and design, creating a sense of excitement among their customer base.

- Mergers and Acquisitions: In the corporate world, mergers and acquisitions involve complex negotiations and discussions. Clear communication is essential to signal the intent behind these business moves. When Google acquired YouTube, both companies communicated the strategic benefits of the merger to their users and stakeholders. The transparency in their communication helped maintain user trust and investor confidence during the transition period.

- Employee Performance Reviews: Effective communication between managers and employees during performance reviews is crucial for setting expectations and goals. By signaling intent, managers can provide constructive feedback, set development plans, and align performance with company objectives. A software company like Adobe uses regular check-ins to discuss career growth and skill development, ensuring that employees are aware of their progress and future prospects within the organization.

Historical Pirate Examples of "Interpersonal Communication: Signaling Intent":

- Hoisting the Black Flag: One of the most iconic signals in pirate history was the hoisting of the black flag, also known as the Jolly Roger. Pirates would raise this flag before attacking another ship, signaling their intent to engage in combat and demand surrender. This straightforward communication left no room for misinterpretation and contributed to the pirates' fearsome reputation.

- Parley: Pirates often used the term "parley" as a signal of intent for peaceful negotiations. When one ship wanted to communicate its desire to discuss terms with another ship, they would raise a white flag and shout "parley." This signaled that they intended to hold a discussion rather than engage in hostilities, promoting the possibility of resolving conflicts without bloodshed.

- Offering Pardon: Some pirate captains, like Bartholomew Roberts, would offer pardons to crews they captured. By communicating their intent to pardon captured sailors who joined their ranks, these pirate leaders enticed potential recruits to join their crew willingly. This approach showcased strategic communication, as it aimed to convert adversaries into allies while ensuring the message was clear and compelling.

4. The Dangers of Ambiguity

In the world of piracy, ambiguity could be a death sentence. A crew uncertain of their captain's intentions or plans was a recipe for disaster. Similarly, in business, ambiguity can be a silent killer. It can lead to misaligned goals, wasted resources, and missed opportunities. Companies that fail to communicate their strategies or change directions without clear communication risk losing the trust of their employees and stakeholders. They also risk being overtaken by competitors who are more decisive and clear in their actions. In a rapidly changing market, ambiguity can leave a company paralyzed, unable to make the necessary decisions to adapt and thrive. The dangers of ambiguity cannot be overstated; it's like sailing in foggy waters without a compass. A company's direction, goals, and strategies need to be communicated clearly and consistently to avoid the pitfalls of ambiguity.

Real World Business Examples of " The Dangers of Ambiguity":

- Apple's Product Launches: Under the leadership of Steve Jobs, Apple became famous for its product launches. Jobs was a master of communication, clearly signaling the company's intent with each new product, from the iPod to the iPhone. These events were not just about unveiling a product but about conveying a clear vision for the future of technology, ensuring that both consumers and shareholders understood Apple's direction and intent.

- Elon Musk's "Master Plan" for Tesla: In 2006, Elon Musk penned a public letter titled "The Secret Tesla Motors Master Plan (just between you and me)." This letter clearly outlined the steps Tesla planned to take over the next decade. By signaling his intent so transparently, Musk set expectations for investors, employees, and customers alike, showcasing where Tesla was headed and what it hoped to achieve.

- Satya Nadella's Vision for Microsoft: When Satya Nadella took over as the CEO of Microsoft, he immediately set about communicating his intent for the company's future. Through memos, public speeches, and actions, he emphasized a shift from a "devices and services" company to a "productivity and platform" company, signaling a renewed focus on cloud computing and collaboration tools. His clear communication realigned the company and has been credited for Microsoft's resurgence in the tech industry.

Historical Pirate Examples of " The Dangers of Ambiguity":

- Captain Kidd's Letters of Marque: Captain William Kidd was a privateer before he was branded a pirate. He operated under "letters of marque," which were licenses issued by governments allowing him to target enemy ships. These letters signaled his intent to other sailors and to any authorities that he was operating legally (at least initially). It was a form of communication to ensure that his actions were seen as legitimate by those who encountered him.

- Pirate Parleys and Truces: Pirates would often meet under a "parley" or a truce to negotiate terms, often signaled by a white flag or another form of communication. This signaled the intent to communicate rather than fight, ensuring both parties understood the nature of the encounter.

- Blackbeard's Slow Match Fuses: Edward Teach, better known as Blackbeard, had a fearsome reputation. One of his tactics was to light slow match fuses in his beard during battle, which created a terrifying image of his face wreathed in smoke. This wasn't just for show—it signaled his intent to be as fearsome and ruthless as possible, discouraging resistance from his enemies.

In both the world of pirates and business, clear communication and signaling intent are crucial for setting expectations, aligning teams, and ensuring successful outcomes. It's not just about stating what will be done but ensuring that others understand and can act in accordance with those intentions.

As we sail to the end of this chapter, let's take a moment, ladies and gents, to reflect on the lessons we've gathered from the high seas and how they're as relevant today in the corporate boardrooms as they were on the decks of pirate ships. The black flag, a symbol of clear intent, serves as a reminder that in any venture, clarity of purpose and communication is paramount. Whether you're leading a team, launching a product, or setting a company's vision, the importance of signaling intent cannot be understated. It's the compass that guides you, ensuring you don't drift off course.

In the corporate world, where competition is fierce and the waters are often murky, hoisting your own 'black flag' of clear intent can be the difference between success and failure. It ensures that your team knows the direction, your stakeholders understand your vision, and your competitors recognize your intent. It's about being transparent, setting clear expectations, and ensuring that everyone is on the same page.

Remember, ambiguity is the enemy of progress. It leads to confusion, misaligned goals, and missed opportunities. So, as you navigate the corporate seas, ensure that your 'black flag' is always hoisted high, signaling your intent to all. And as Captain Martin Marlinspike would say, "In business, as in piracy, clarity is the key to success." So, keep your sails taut, your compass true, and always be clear in your intent. Until our next adventure, may your seas be calm and your ventures prosperous. Safe voyages, my darlings!

Chapter 10: "The Pirate's Parley" - The Art of Negotiation and Alliance in Business

Yo Ho Yo Ho!, dear readers! As we embark on this chapter of our grand voyage through the vast oceans of business, the tales of pirates, with their audacity, cunning, and adventure, beckon us. These seafarers, often perceived as mere treasure hunters and rebels, were in fact astute strategists, negotiators, and leaders. Their world, filled with legends, myths, and real-life adventures, offers a rich tapestry of lessons that find deep resonance in today's dynamic business landscape. I am Captain Martin Marlinspike, your seasoned guide, and I've witnessed firsthand the parallels between the high seas and boardrooms, between pirate parleys and corporate negotiations.

The world of piracy, with its unpredictable tides and treacherous storms, serves as a vivid metaphor for the modern business realm. Just as pirates had to navigate these challenges, today's business leaders face their own set of trials. From rapidly changing market dynamics to fierce competition, from technological disruptions to evolving consumer preferences, the challenges are manifold. But within these challenges lie opportunities, waiting to be seized by those with the vision, the strategy, and the audacity to chart their own course. And who better to guide us through these tumultuous waters than the pirates of old, with their tales of daring, strategy, and innovation?

Now, one might wonder, what do the tales of pirates, with their codes, their parleys, and their adventures, have to do with the world of business? The answer lies in the timeless lessons they offer. Pirates, contrary to popular belief, weren't always about brute force. Many a time, they relied on their wit, charm, and negotiation skills to strike deals, form alliances, and avoid unnecessary conflicts. Their ability to adapt, to read the winds and the waves, and to make decisions on the fly, offers invaluable insights for businesses. In a world that's constantly changing, where the only constant is change itself, the ability to adapt, to innovate, and to stay ahead of the curve is more crucial than ever.

So, as we delve deeper into this chapter, guided by the wisdom of pirates and their tales from the high seas, let's uncover the secrets of effective negotiation, the art of alliance, and the importance of trust and compromise. Let's set sail on this journey, with the stars to guide us and the wind in our sails, as we explore the vast oceans of business, guided by the timeless

1. Understanding the Stakes: Knowing What's on the Line

In the world of piracy, every negotiation had high stakes. Whether it was dividing the spoils of a raid, deciding the fate of captured prisoners, or forging alliances for future endeavors, pirates had to be acutely aware of what was on the line. This awareness informed their strategy, their approach, and their willingness to compromise. Similarly, in business, understanding the stakes is crucial. Whether you're negotiating a merger, striking a deal with a supplier, or forging a partnership with a competitor, being aware of what's at stake for all lessons from the world of piracy.

Figure 15- Midjourney(2023)

parties involved can give you an edge. It allows you to approach the negotiation with clarity, purpose, and a clear strategy.

Real World Business Examples of "Understanding the Stakes: Knowing What's on the Line":

- Disney's Acquisition of Pixar: In 2006, Disney purchased Pixar for $7.4 billion. At the time, Disney's own animation studio was struggling, while Pixar had a string of hits. Disney recognized the stakes: the future of animated films, the value of intellectual property, and the need to rejuvenate its animation dominance. Bob Iger, Disney's CEO, understood that by bringing Pixar into the Disney fold, they would not only acquire valuable IPs but also the creative genius behind Pixar's success. (Chaffin & Poliiti, 2006)

- Microsoft's Entry into the Console Market with Xbox: Microsoft's decision to enter the gaming console market was a high-stakes gamble. They were going up against well-established players like Sony's PlayStation and Nintendo. Understanding what was on the line (a piece of the lucrative gaming market and ensuring a foothold in living rooms globally), Microsoft invested heavily in the Xbox's development, its game library, and marketing. (Karmali, 2013)

- Blockbuster's Decline and Netflix's Rise: Blockbuster failed to understand the stakes when they had an opportunity to buy Netflix for a mere $50 million in 2000. Not recognizing the future of streaming and the shifting dynamics of movie rentals, Blockbuster missed out, leading to its eventual downfall. On the other hand, Netflix knew that the stakes were about dominating the future of entertainment consumption and pivoted from a DVD-by-mail service to a streaming powerhouse. (MISRA, 2020)

Historical Pirate Examples of "Understanding the Stakes: Knowing What's on the Line":

- Black Bart's Code: Bartholomew Roberts, also known as Black Bart, was one of history's most successful pirates. Understanding the stakes involved in maintaining order and loyalty among his crew, he established a pirate code. This set of rules ensured fair division of spoils and set punishments for misdeeds. By setting clear expectations, he maintained a cohesive crew which was critical given the constant dangers of the pirate lifestyle.

- Captain Kidd's Trial: When Captain William Kidd was captured and put on trial, he believed that certain influential backers in England would support him, thinking the stakes for them were their reputations and investments. However, they distanced themselves, and Kidd was hanged. The real stakes were political, as the ruling elite needed to show they were tough on piracy.

- Pirate Havens in Madagascar and Nassau: Pirates often sought out safe havens, like Madagascar and Nassau, where they could resupply, sell their loot, and rest. These havens were crucial because pirates knew the stakes: without safe harbors, they would be vulnerable to naval forces and bounty hunters. These sanctuaries allowed pirates to continue their operations and remain a step ahead of those pursuing them.

Both in the world of piracy and business, understanding the stakes is essential. It provides a clear perspective on potential gains and losses, informing strategies and decisions. By appreciating what's on the line, individuals and organizations can navigate situations more effectively and emerge victorious.

2. The Power of Information: Knowledge as Leverage

Pirates, when entering negotiations, often sought to gather as much information as possible. Knowing the strengths, weaknesses, and motivations of the other party provided leverage, allowing pirates to negotiate from a position of strength. They would often send scouts or spies to gather intelligence or use their network of informants to get the information they needed. In the business world, information is power. Before entering any negotiation, it's crucial to gather as much information as possible about the other party. This knowledge can provide insights into their motivations, their pain points, and their objectives, allowing you to tailor your approach and strategy accordingly.

- **The Silent Observers:** Pirates' scouts were their eyes and ears, covertly gathering intel without drawing attention. In a similar vein, businesses today have tools like market research, data analytics, and competitive analysis to silently observe market trends, customer behaviors, and competitor moves. These tools, when used effectively, can provide a competitive edge.

- **Leveraging Social Dynamics:** Pirates understood that sometimes the most valuable information came from eavesdropping on tavern conversations or leveraging interpersonal relationships. In the corporate setting, understanding the social dynamics of an organization or industry can offer profound insights. Engaging in networking, attending industry conferences, or even informal chats can reveal information not found in formal reports.

- **Beyond Raw Data:** While pirates relied on facts, like the size and firepower of an opponent's ship, they also delved into psychological insights, gauging the morale and intent of rival crews. Businesses too must realize that while quantitative data is vital, qualitative insights – understanding motivations, cultural nuances, and emotional drivers – can be equally crucial in negotiations.

- **Protecting Your Treasure Trove:** Just as pirates safeguarded their maps and intel, businesses must ensure the security of their data. In a world where cyber threats are ever-present, protecting sensitive information is paramount. A leak can not only lead to competitive disadvantages but also erode trust among stakeholders.

- **Ethics in Espionage:** While gathering information is essential, it's crucial to adhere to ethical standards. Pirates, despite their lawless image, often had their own moral codes. Corporate espionage, insider trading, or other illicit means of obtaining information can lead to severe repercussions, both legally and reputationally.

Information, when harnessed correctly, is one of the most potent tools in a negotiator's arsenal. But as with any tool, its effectiveness lies in the hands of its user. Business leaders, like the shrewd pirates of yesteryears, must understand the nuances of gathering, interpreting, and utilizing information, ensuring they sail smoothly through negotiations, armed with knowledge and insight.

Real World Business Examples of "The Power of Information: Knowledge as Leverage":

- Apple's Secrecy and Product Launches: Apple is notorious for its tight-lipped approach to product development. By controlling information about upcoming products, Apple ensures maximum impact during product launches. Competitors are left in the dark, giving Apple a distinct advantage in market positioning and product differentiation.

- Google's Acquisition of YouTube: In 2006, Google acquired YouTube for $1.65 billion. Google, understanding the importance of video in the future of the internet, leveraged its vast resources and data to identify YouTube's potential. Their insight into user behavior and online trends gave them the knowledge they needed to make a strategic acquisition that would later dominate online video streaming. (Allison & Van Duyn, 2006)

- Walmart's Supply Chain Management: Walmart is a master of supply chain optimization, primarily because of its data-driven approach. By meticulously tracking sales, inventory, and customer behavior, Walmart can forecast demand, streamline its supply chain, and drive efficiencies. This information gives Walmart an edge over competitors, allowing it to offer lower prices and maintain its dominant market position. (Souza, 2021)

Historical Pirate Examples of "The Power of Information: Knowledge as Leverage":

- Captain Kidd and the Quedagh Merchant: In 1698, Captain William Kidd captured the Quedagh Merchant, a ship rich with treasures. Kidd had information that the ship was traveling without its usual convoy, making it vulnerable. Leveraging this information, Kidd and his crew seized the vessel, one of the most significant captures of his career.

- Anne Bonny and Mary Read's Deception: Two of the most famous female pirates, Anne Bonny and Mary Read, often disguised themselves as men. By gathering information about how male pirates behaved and leveraging the surprise element, they could more effectively engage in combat and piracy, catching their adversaries off guard.

- Pirate Spies in Port Towns: Pirates often had informants in major port towns who would relay information about departing ships, their cargo, and their routes. With this knowledge, pirates could strategically position their ships for ambush, ensuring a higher success rate in their raids.

- In both piracy and business, having the right information at the right time can be a game-changer. Leveraging knowledge effectively allows for strategic decision-making, ensuring that actions are informed, calculated, and have a higher probability of success.

3. The Art of Compromise: Finding Common Ground

While pirates had a reputation for ruthlessness, they also understood the value of compromise. Not every disagreement had to end in a sword fight. Often, finding common ground and striking a mutually beneficial deal was more advantageous. They knew that sometimes it was better to share the spoils than to lose everything in a battle. In business, the ability to compromise, to find common ground, and to strike a balance between competing interests is invaluable. While it's essential to have clear objectives and red lines, being too rigid can lead to missed opportunities. Effective negotiators know when to hold firm and when to compromise.

Real World Business Examples of "The Art of Compromise: Finding Common Ground":

Disney and Pixar: In the early 2000s, the relationship between Disney and Pixar was strained, with disputes over profit-sharing and control of sequels. However, rather than parting ways and potentially harming both companies, they found common ground. In 2006, Disney acquired Pixar for $7.4 billion, leading to a collaboration that produced some of the

- most successful animated films in history, like "Up" and "Toy Story 3." (Orr, 2017)

- Microsoft and Linux: For years, Microsoft viewed open-source software, particularly Linux, as a threat to its business. However, in a notable compromise and shift in strategy, Microsoft began to embrace Linux and open-source in general. By 2020, Linux was fully integrated into Windows 10, allowing developers to run a full Linux kernel within Windows.

This compromise not only benefited Microsoft but also the broader developer community. (Maruccia, 2022)

- Boeing and Airbus Emissions Agreement: Historically fierce competitors, Boeing and Airbus, recognized the growing concern about aircraft emissions. Instead of individually trying to tackle the issue or using it as a competitive edge, both companies compromised in 2011 to work together on developing sustainable biofuels to reduce aviation's carbon footprint. (Reuters, 2008)

Historical Pirate Examples of "The Art of Compromise: Finding Common Ground":

- Pirate Alliances: Pirates like Bartholomew Roberts and Calico Jack occasionally formed alliances. Instead of competing for the same prizes and potentially clashing with one another, they would strike agreements to work together or divide areas of operation, ensuring that both could profit without interference.

- Pirates and Pirate Havens: Pirates needed safe places to repair ships, recruit crew, and sell stolen goods. Places like Port Royal in Jamaica became known as pirate havens, where local authorities would compromise with pirates, allowing them safe harbor in exchange for a cut of the profits or protection from other threats.

- Pirate Codes and Ship Democracy: Many pirate ships operated with a form of democracy where major decisions were put to a vote among the crew. This system forced compromise, as decisions had to account for the desires and concerns of the majority. The pirate code, or ship's articles, would often set out rules for distribution of booty, behavior on the ship, and compensation for injuries, ensuring that all crew members had a voice and that disputes could be settled without resorting to violence.

In both the worlds of piracy and business, recognizing the value in collaboration and compromise can lead to outcomes that are beneficial for all parties involved.

4. Building Trust: The Foundation of Lasting Alliances

Pirates, despite their reputation, often had to rely on trust. Whether it was trusting their crew, their allies, or even their rivals during a negotiation, trust was a valuable commodity on the high seas. They knew that a crew that didn't trust its captain was more likely to mutiny, and an ally that didn't trust you was more likely to betray you. In the world of business, trust is the foundation of any successful negotiation or alliance. Building trust, honoring commitments, and demonstrating integrity can open doors, create opportunities, and lead to lasting partnerships.
Real World Business Examples of "Building Trust: The Foundation of Lasting Alliances":

Apple and IBM: Historically, these two tech giants were bitter rivals in the 1980s. However, in 2014 they surprised many by forming a partnership to create enterprise solutions that leveraged the strengths of both companies. Their alliance was built on mutual trust and a shared vision of reshaping business technology. This move demonstrated that past

Figure 17- Midjourney(2023)

- competition doesn't prevent future collaboration if there's trust. (Colt, 2014)

- Toyota and BMW: In 2013, these automobile giants announced a collaboration to share technology and knowledge. Despite being competitors, they built trust by respecting each other's strengths and started joint ventures in areas like battery technology and sports car development. This trust-based alliance allowed both companies to benefit from shared innovation. (Burgess, 2016)

- Netflix and Comcast: Initially, these two companies were at odds, particularly around the topic of net neutrality. However, recognizing the mutual benefits, they struck a deal in 2014 where Netflix agreed to pay Comcast for direct access to its broadband network, ensuring a smoother service for Netflix subscribers. This deal, built on trust, showed that even companies with past disagreements can form alliances if it benefits their customers. (MISRA, 2020)

Historical Pirate Examples of "Building Trust: The Foundation of Lasting Alliances":

- Blackbeard and Stede Bonnet: Blackbeard, a seasoned pirate, formed an unlikely alliance with Stede Bonnet, a former army major turned pirate. Though their backgrounds and experiences were vastly different, they built a trust that saw them jointly raiding ships along the American coast. Their partnership exemplified how trust could bring together even the most unlikely of allies.

- Pirate Republic of Nassau: In the early 18th century, pirates formed a sort of republic in Nassau, Bahamas. These pirates, despite their individual ambitions and backgrounds, built a system based on mutual trust. The Pirate Republic had its code and systems of governance, showing that even in a society built on lawlessness, trust was the key to cohesion.

- Anne Bonny and Mary Read: Two of the most famous female pirates, Anne Bonny and Mary Read, formed a tight bond built on trust when they were part of Calico Jack's crew. Their alliance was so strong that during one battle, when their ship was attacked and the male crew members hid, these two women stood their ground, showcasing the strength of their trust-based partnership.

In both piracy and business, establishing trust can lead to strong and often unexpected alliances, proving its pivotal role in successful partnerships.

As we drop anchor at the end of this enlightening chapter, it's essential to take a moment to reflect on the myriad lessons the audacious world of piracy offers to the modern business realm. The high seas, with their unpredictable tides, treacherous storms, and the ever-present danger from rival pirates, serve as a vivid metaphor for today's dynamic business landscape. Just as pirates had to navigate these challenges with wit, cunning, and strategy, today's business leaders must also chart their course with foresight, adaptability, and a keen understanding of the stakes involved. Captain Martin Marlinspike, with his vast experience of both worlds, often muses, "The sea, much like the business world, is unforgiving to those unprepared. But for those who are ready, who have the right mix of audacity and strategy, it offers treasures beyond measure."

The tales of pirates, filled with high-stakes negotiations, strategic alliances, and the ever-important element of trust, provide a treasure trove of insights. These seafarers, often operating on the fringes of society, understood the importance of building and maintaining trust. They knew that a crew that didn't trust its captain was more likely to mutiny, and an ally that didn't trust you was more likely to turn foe. In the same vein, in the world of business, trust forms the bedrock of any successful venture. Whether it's between a company and its customers, between business partners, or between an employer and employees, trust is the glue that holds everything together. It's the foundation upon which lasting relationships are built, and it's the key to long-term success.

Furthermore, the art of negotiation, as practiced by pirates, offers invaluable lessons. They knew when to hold firm, when to compromise, and when to walk away. They understood the value of information, of understanding the other party's motivations, strengths, and weaknesses. In today's business world, where deals are struck every second, where mergers, acquisitions, and partnerships are the order of the day, the ability to negotiate effectively is more crucial than ever. It's an art that requires a delicate balance of assertiveness and empathy, of understanding and strategy. As you, dear reader, continue on your business journey, may you always remember the lessons from this chapter. May you navigate the challenges with the audacity of a pirate, forge alliances with the wisdom of a seasoned captain, and build trust with the integrity of a true leader.

In the end, as we prepare to set sail to our next destination, remember that the world of business, much like the high seas, is vast, unpredictable, and full of opportunities. It's a world where the lessons from the past, from the audacious exploits of pirates, can light the way to a brighter, more prosperous future. So, hoist your sails, set your course, and embark on your next adventure with the wisdom of the ages as your guiding star. Until our next chapter, may the winds always be in your favor, and may your journey be filled with success, adventure, and endless possibilities.

Chapter 11: " A smooth sea never made for a skilled sailor" - Embracing Challenges for Growth and Resilience

Avast ye intrepid explorers of knowledge and wisdom! Welcome to a chapter that sails through the unpredictable currents of adaptation—a chapter that draws inspiration from the brave souls who navigated uncharted waters with unwavering determination. I am Captain Martin Marlinspike, your companion on this voyage, and together, we shall delve deep into the realm of adaptability, where historical tales of pirates and the modern world of business intertwine.

Picture a ship at sea, its sails billowing against the wind, its crew ready to face whatever tumultuous waves the ocean throws their way. Just as pirates relied on their skills to adjust their course when faced with unpredictable currents, so too do businesses in the dynamic landscape of today. The ability to adapt swiftly and strategically is no longer just an advantage; it's a necessity for survival. From historical pirates who deftly changed course to modern companies that pivot in response to market shifts, the importance of adaptability stands as a guiding light in both tumultuous seas and turbulent markets.

In the annals of history, pirates like Captain Kidd and Blackbeard were revered for their remarkable adaptability in the face of uncertainty. They understood that the sea was an ever-changing mistress, and to thrive, one must learn to read the currents and adjust the sails accordingly. Fast forward to the present, and the business landscape is no less challenging.

Companies like Netflix have revolutionized industries by embracing change and boldly steering into uncharted territories. The stories of pirates and the strategies of modern entrepreneurs converge to remind us that the ability to adapt isn't just a skill—it's a mindset that shapes destinies, both on the high seas and in the boardrooms of today.

As we embark on this voyage through the tides of adaptation, prepare to discover the lessons and insights that historical pirates offer us. We'll explore the tales of captains who navigated through adversity, harnessed opportunities from challenges, and emerged victorious. Alongside these stories, we'll chart the course of modern businesses that have harnessed the power of adaptability to rise above the waves of change and disruption. Together, let us unlock the secrets of agility and resilience, and emerge with a deeper understanding of the currents that shape success and growth in both history and the business realm. So, my fellow adventurers, hoist the sails of curiosity, and let the winds of adaptability carry us through the chapters ahead.

1. Cultivating a Growth Mindset

Pirates understood that challenges were opportunities to learn, adapt, and improve. Every stormy encounter with the sea presented a chance to refine their navigation skills and hone their ability to make split-second decisions. The pirate Blackbeard, renowned for his strategic prowess, thrived on the complexity of challenges, transforming them into learning experiences that made him a formidable adversary.

In the business realm, companies like Microsoft prioritize a growth mindset among their employees. Microsoft's CEO, Satya Nadella, encourages a culture that embraces challenges and views them as opportunities for growth. By fostering a mindset that values learning from failures and setbacks, Microsoft has nurtured a workforce that remains resilient and adaptable in the face of change.

Real World Business Examples of "Cultivating a Growth Mindset":

- Microsoft's Growth Mindset Culture: Microsoft is a prime example of a company that prioritizes a growth mindset. Under the leadership of CEO Satya Nadella, the company has shifted its culture to embrace challenges as opportunities for growth and learning. Nadella's "growth mindset" philosophy encourages employees to approach challenges with curiosity and view failures as stepping stones toward improvement. This shift has led to innovations like Microsoft Azure, a cloud computing platform, and the transformation of Microsoft Office into a subscription-based service. By fostering a culture that values continuous learning and adaptation, Microsoft has maintained its relevance and competitiveness in the rapidly evolving technology landscape. (Tabrizi, 2023)

- 2. Google's 20% Time: Google's famous "20% time" policy is another example of cultivating a growth mindset. Google encourages employees to spend 20% of their work time on personal projects that interest them, even if those projects aren't directly related to their roles. This policy has led to the creation of innovative products like Gmail and Google News. By allowing employees to explore their passions and experiment with new ideas, Google fosters a culture of continuous learning, innovation, and personal growth. (Clark, 2022)

- 3. Netflix's Approach to Disruption: Netflix's journey from a DVD rental service to a global streaming platform demonstrates a growth mindset in action. When faced with the disruption of the entertainment industry and the decline of physical media, Netflix adapted and embraced the streaming revolution. The company recognized the need to innovate and pivot its business model, leading to its success as a dominant player in the digital entertainment landscape. By viewing challenges as opportunities to evolve and transform, Netflix has become a prime example of a company that thrives on a growth-oriented mindset. (MISRA, 2020)

Historical Pirate Examples of " Cultivating a Growth Mindset ":

- Blackbeard's Tactical Brilliance: The pirate Blackbeard, known as Edward Teach, was a master of strategy and tactics. He cultivated a growth mindset by viewing every encounter with naval forces as a chance to learn and adapt. Blackbeard's audacity and ability to strategize effectively allowed him to commandeer and repurpose captured vessels for his fleet. His approach to challenges as opportunities for growth made him a formidable adversary in the Golden Age of Piracy.

- Calico Jack's Resourcefulness: Calico Jack Rackham, a notorious pirate, embodied a growth mindset by continuously adapting to changing circumstances. When his ship, the "Revenge," was seized by the British Navy, he swiftly acquired a new vessel and continued his piratical endeavors. Calico Jack's ability to bounce back from setbacks and see challenges as chances to innovate and evolve showcased his growth-oriented mindset.

- Mary Read's Disguise and Adaptation: Mary Read, a pioneering female pirate, demonstrated a growth mindset through her ability to adapt to her environment. Disguised as a man, Mary Read sailed alongside male pirates, adapting to the gender norms of the time to pursue her passion for piracy. Her willingness to embrace challenges and navigate complex social dynamics illustrated her growth mindset and determination to thrive in a male-dominated field.

The parallel between historical pirates' approaches to challenges and modern businesses' emphasis on cultivating a growth mindset underscores the timeless importance of viewing obstacles as opportunities for learning, improvement, and innovation.

2. Adapting to Unpredictable Currents

Pirates faced ever-changing conditions on the open sea, from sudden storms to uncharted waters. Their ability to adapt swiftly was essential for survival. Pirate crews like Captain Kidd's were known for their capacity to navigate through unpredictable currents and uncharted territories, demonstrating a level of adaptability that set them apart.

Similarly, in the business world, companies like Netflix epitomize adaptability. By pivoting from a DVD rental service to a streaming platform, Netflix navigated the shifting currents of technology and consumer preferences. Their ability to embrace change and reinvent themselves showcases the power of adaptability in ensuring long-term success.

Real World Business Examples of "Adapting to Unpredictable Currents":

- Netflix's Transformation: Netflix's transition from a DVD rental service to a streaming powerhouse is a prime example of adaptability. As technology and consumer behavior evolved, Netflix recognized the changing currents of the entertainment industry. The company adapted swiftly by embracing the streaming model, creating original content, and catering to on-demand viewing preferences. This adaptability not only saved Netflix from potential obsolescence but also propelled it to become a dominant player in the digital streaming landscape. (MISRA, 2020)

- Amazon's Evolution: Amazon's journey from an online bookstore to an e-commerce juggernaut showcases remarkable adaptability. As the company expanded its offerings to include a wide range of products and services, it demonstrated an innate ability to adjust to the ever-changing currents of consumer demands. Amazon's introduction of Prime membership, which provides fast shipping and access to digital content, reflects its commitment to adapting to evolving customer expectations and preferences. (DePillis & Sherman, 2018)

- Tesla's Shift in Focus: Tesla's shift from being solely an electric car manufacturer to a comprehensive clean energy company illustrates adaptability in the face of changing market dynamics. Recognizing the growing demand for sustainable energy solutions, Tesla expanded its offerings to include solar panels, energy storage solutions, and electric vehicle charging infrastructure. This strategic shift demonstrates the company's ability to navigate unpredictable currents and position itself as a leader in the sustainable energy sector.

Historical Pirate Examples of "Adapting to Unpredictable Currents":

- Captain Bartholomew Roberts' Adaptability: Captain Bartholomew Roberts, a feared pirate of the early 18th century, demonstrated remarkable adaptability in his tactics. When confronted by a French warship while raiding the coast of Guinea, Roberts and his crew successfully maneuvered their ship in treacherous waters to escape capture. His ability to adapt to unexpected challenges and navigate dangerous waters showcased his exceptional skill as a pirate captain.

- Captain John Quelch's Uncharted Territories: Captain John Quelch, a notorious pirate of the late 17th century, navigated uncharted waters with resourcefulness. After capturing a Portuguese ship laden with valuable cargo, Quelch recognized the need to hide his plundered riches. He sailed to the remote island of New Hampshire to bury his treasure, showcasing his adaptability in finding unconventional solutions to challenges. (Simmons University, n.d.)

- 3. Pirate Anne Bonny's Survival Instincts: Pirate Anne Bonny's life as a female pirate in the early 18th century required constant adaptation. Disguised as a man, she navigated the complex social dynamics of pirate crews. When her ship was captured by the Royal Navy, Bonny's ability to adapt saved her from execution; her pregnancy spared her life. Her capacity to adjust to the unpredictable currents of pirate life demonstrated her survival instincts and resourcefulness.

The convergence of historical pirates' nimble responses to challenges and modern businesses' emphasis on adaptability underscores the timeless significance of adjusting swiftly to changing circumstances. Just as pirates deftly navigated the uncharted seas, successful businesses navigate the currents of evolving industries and consumer demands to thrive and remain relevant.

3. Building Resilience Through Challenges

Pirates understood that resilience was born from facing challenges head-on. The pirate Anne Bonny, known for her fiery spirit, endured adversity with unwavering determination. Her resilience in the face of danger and uncertainty showcased her ability to emerge stronger from challenges.

In today's corporate landscape, companies like Starbucks have demonstrated resilience by adapting to unexpected challenges. During the 2008 recession, Starbucks faced declining sales but emerged stronger by focusing on innovation, improving customer experiences, and streamlining operations. This ability to weather storms and emerge with renewed vigor exemplifies the spirit of resilience.

Figure 19- Midjourney(2023)

As we bring this chapter to a close, we find ourselves on the shores of a profound truth: the art of adapting to unpredictable currents isn't just a skill—it's a mindset that separates the ordinary from the extraordinary, the stagnant from the thriving. The stories of historical pirates and the examples from the modern business world intertwine to paint a vivid picture of the significance of adaptability in the face of ever-changing tides.

In the swift currents of the business realm, companies that fail to adapt risk being left behind by the relentless waves of innovation and changing consumer preferences. The historical pirates' ability to navigate through uncharted waters and unforeseen challenges serves as a timeless reminder that adaptability isn't a luxury; it's a necessity for survival. Just as pirates recognized that the sea could be both a source of danger and opportunity, modern businesses must embrace change as a chance to rise above adversity and steer toward success.

The power of adaptability extends beyond mere survival—it's a catalyst for growth and prosperity. Companies like Netflix, Amazon, and Tesla have shown that by embracing change, reinventing themselves, and seizing emerging opportunities, they not only weather storms but also thrive in the wake of disruption. These examples echo the stories of pirates who transformed challenges into opportunities and adversity into triumph. Like the pirate crews that maneuvered through treacherous waters, successful businesses must possess the agility and willingness to alter their course, adjust their strategies, and harness the winds of change to propel them forward.

In the final analysis, the age-old wisdom of pirates and the modern lessons of adaptability converge to illuminate a universal truth: the ability to adapt to unpredictable currents is a hallmark of greatness. Whether sailing the high seas or navigating the complex currents of the business world, the resilient and agile are the ones who not only survive but thrive. As you embark on your own journey, let the echoes of historical pirates and the innovative spirits of modern businesses guide you in embracing change, navigating uncertainty, and charting a course to success in the ever-changing waters of life and business.

Bibliography

Álvarez, J. (2020, 06 19). Retrieved from
    https://www.labrujulaverde.com/en/2020/06/bartolomeu-
    portugues-the-lusitanian-buccaneer-who-created-the-code-
    of-piracy/

Allison, K., & Van Duyn, A. (2006, 10 09). Retrieved from
    https://www.ft.com/content/5818fb64-579b-11db-be9f-
    0000779e2340

Apple. (2007, 01 09). Retrieved from
    https://www.apple.com/newsroom/2007/01/09Apple-
    Reinvents-the-Phone-with-iPhone/

Banerji, U. (2022, 06 15). Retrieved from
    https://www.atlasobscura.com/articles/ching-shih-chinese-
    female-pirate

Blystone, D. (2023, 4 18). Retrieved from
    https://www.investopedia.com/articles/personal-
    finance/111015/story-uber.asp

Britannica. (n.d.). Retrieved from
    https://www.britannica.com/biography/Francis-Drake

Burgess, A. (2016, 08 03). Retrieved from
    https://www.themanufacturer.com/articles/bmw-and-toyota-
    combine-to-create-their-latest-sports-cars/

Burnison, G. (2019, 02 28). Retrieved from
    https://www.cnbc.com/2019/02/28/what-google-learned-in-
    its-quest-to-build-the-perfect-team.html

capitalism.com. (2022, 11 17). Retrieved from
    https://www.capitalism.com/history-of-amazon/

Cartwright, M. (2021, 09 15). Retrieved from
    https://www.worldhistory.org/Henry_Every/

Cartwright, M. (2021, 09 07). Retrieved from
https://www.worldhistory.org/Bartholomew_Roberts/

Cartwright, M. (2021, 09 25). Retrieved from
https://www.worldhistory.org/Captain_Kidd/

CBS News. (2015, 11 09). Retrieved from
https://www.cbsnews.com/news/starbucks-minimalist-
holiday-cup-war-on-christmas/

Chadwick, J. (2023, 04 20). Retrieved from
https://www.dailymail.co.uk/sciencetech/article-
11989749/How-Netflixs-DVD-rental-business-transformed-
way-people-watched-TV-movies-home.html

Chaffin, J., & Poliiti, J. (2006, 01 24). Retrieved from
https://www.ft.com/content/3c946d16-8cde-11da-9daf-
0000779e2340

Clark, D. (2022, 01 07). Retrieved from
https://www.cnbc.com/2021/12/16/google-20-percent-rule-
shows-exactly-how-much-time-you-should-spend-learning-
new-skills.html

Clay, E. (2020, 11 10). Retrieved from https://independent-
photo.com/news/historic-brands-kodak/

coca-cola. (n.d.). Retrieved from https://www.coca-
colacompany.com/about-us/history/new-coke-the-most-
memorable-marketing-blunder-ever

Colt, S. (2014, 07 15). Retrieved from
https://www.businessinsider.com/apple-ibm-enterprise-
partnership-2014-7

DePillis, L., & Sherman, I. (2018). Retrieved from
https://www.cnn.com/interactive/2018/10/business/amazon-
history-timeline/index.html

Eassa, A. (2019, 04 15). Retrieved from
https://www.fool.com/investing/2019/02/11/heres-how-
qualcomm-makes-its-money.aspx

Entrepreneur.com. (2008, 10 10). Retrieved from
        https://www.entrepreneur.com/growing-a-business/anita-
        roddicks-biography/197688

Fabry, M. (2018, 05 04). Retrieved from
        https://time.com/5252406/ben-jerry-ice-cream-40/

Fernandez-Armesto, E. B. (n.d.). Retrieved from
        https://www.britannica.com/biography/Francis-Drake

Finley, K. (2016, 04 27). Retrieved from
        https://www.wired.com/2016/04/hey-nokia-isnt-just-
        company-used-make-phones/

Fortune. (2022, 6 28). *Fortune.com*. Retrieved from
        https://fortune.com/2022/06/28/warren-buffett-wealth-
        estate-family-charity/

Frampton, S. (2020, 03 13). Retrieved from
        https://chattermill.com/blog/zappos-customer-service

Frommer, D. (2011, 06 06). Retrieved from
        https://www.businessinsider.com/iphone-android-
        smartphones-2011-6

Garza, A. D. (2023, 07 20). Retrieved from
        https://time.com/6296007/beyond-meat-steak-ceo-
        interview/

Gibbons, S. (2019, 05 21). Retrieved from
        https://www.forbes.com/sites/serenitygibbons/2019/05/21/
        what-the-rise-of-netflixs-original-content-can-teach-leaders-
        about-diversity/?sh=9ee43ec7a56b

Griffith, E. (2018, 04 03). Retrieved from
        https://www.wired.com/story/spotify-and-the-triumph-of-
        the-subscription-model/

Hargreaves, R. (2019, 04 30). Retrieved from
        https://www.yahoo.com/video/warren-buffetts-due-
        diligence-process-163515755.html

history.co.uk. (n.d.). Retrieved from
        https://www.history.co.uk/articles/the-life-of-pirate-calcio-
        jack-rackham

Karmali, L. (2013, 02 06). Retrieved from
https://www.ign.com/articles/2013/02/06/why-microsoft-
got-into-the-console-business

Kastrenakes, J. (2018, 06 27). Retrieved from
https://www.theverge.com/2018/6/27/17510908/apple-
samsung-settle-patent-battle-over-copying-iphone

Knight, J. (1982, 10 11). Retrieved from
https://www.washingtonpost.com/archive/business/1982/10
/11/tylenols-maker-shows-how-to-respond-to-
crisis/bc8df898-3fcf-443f-bc2f-e6fbd639a5a3/

Lee, T. B. (2013, 10 25). Retrieved from
https://www.washingtonpost.com/news/the-
switch/wp/2013/10/25/15-years-ago-congress-kept-mickey-
mouse-out-of-the-public-domain-will-they-do-it-again/

Leswing, K. (2021, 11 13). Retrieved from
https://www.cnbc.com/2021/11/13/apples-privacy-changes-
show-the-power-it-holds-over-other-industries.html

LEWIS, A. (2021, 12 07). *www.sequoiacap.com*. Retrieved from
https://www.sequoiacap.com/article/brian-chesky-airbnb-
spotlight/

Manangi, S. (2017, 07 31). Retrieved from
https://www.linkedin.com/pulse/ubers-global-expansion-
strategy-think-local-expand-work-manangi/

marshadelamothe. (2023, 06 14). Retrieved from
https://signsmystery.com/pirate-flags-communication/

Maruccia, A. (2022, 10 23). Retrieved from
https://www.techspot.com/news/96753-windows-subsystem-
linux-comes-microsoft-store-everyone.html

MasterClass. (2022, 08 30). Retrieved from
https://www.masterclass.com/articles/sara-blakely-founder-
of-spanx

McCord, P. (2014, 01). Retrieved from https://hbr.org/2014/01/how-
netflix-reinvented-hr

Midjourney. (2023). Retrieved from Midjourney (V5) [Text-to-image]:
https://www.midjourney.com/

Miller, K. (2009). Retrieved from https://www.webmd.com/a-to-z-
guides/features/off-label-drug-use-what-you-need-to-know

Milligan, M. (2022, 01 19). Retrieved from
https://www.heritagedaily.com/2022/01/the-pirate-
code/142542

Minster, C. (2019, 05 30). Retrieved from
https://www.thoughtco.com/pirate-ships-overview-
2136229#:~:text=The%20pirates%20usually%20changed%20t
he,cargo)%20onboard%20than%20merchant's%20vessels.

MISRA, A. (2020, 09 13). Retrieved from The Strategy Story:
https://thestrategystory.com/2020/09/13/netflix-pivoting-
business-model/

Moorman, C. (2018, 09 23). Retrieved from
https://www.forbes.com/sites/christinemoorman/2018/08/2
3/adobe-how-to-dominate-the-subscription-
economy/?sh=2fd3aee652e8

Mupeti, L. (2023, 04 24). Retrieved from
https://www.linkedin.com/pulse/legacy-think-different-how-
apples-campaign-continues-inspire-mupeti/

National Parks Service. (2020, 09 22). Retrieved from
https://www.nps.gov/jela/learn/historyculture/jean-lafitte-
history-mystery.htm

Neiger, C. (2022, 09 30). Retrieved from
https://www.fool.com/investing/2022/09/30/tesla-is-right-to-
sell-directly-to-consumers-heres/

Newsweek. (1993, 06 27). Retrieved from
https://www.newsweek.com/great-pepsi-panic-193794

NY Times. (2000, 02 22). Retrieved from
https://www.nytimes.com/2000/02/22/science/seeking-
pirate-treasure-captain-kidd-s-sunken-ship.html

NY Times. (2002, 03 23). Retrieved from
https://www.nytimes.com/2002/03/23/your-money/IHT-

tylenol-made-a-hero-of-johnson-johnson-the-recall-that-started.html

Orr, C. (2017, 06). Retrieved from https://www.theatlantic.com/magazine/archive/2017/06/how-pixar-lost-its-way/524484/

O'Sullivan, F., & Loudis, J. (2023, 08 02). Retrieved from https://www.bloomberg.com/news/features/2023-08-02/cities-keep-trying-and-failing-to-regulate-airbnb-nasdaq-abnb

Peterson, H. (2016, 02 03). Retrieved from https://www.businessinsider.com/kfc-mutant-chicken-rumors-are-not-real-2016-2

piratesofnassau.com. (n.d.). Retrieved from http://www.piratesofnassau.com/the-republic-of-pirates/

Princeton.edu. (n.d.). Retrieved from https://lib-dbserver.princeton.edu/visual_materials/maps/websites/pacific/dampier/dampier.html

Restrepo, M. L. (2022, 10 06). Retrieved from https://www.npr.org/2022/10/06/1127032721/nike-just-do-it-slogan-success-dan-wieden-kennedy-dies#:~:text=In%20an%20interview%20with%20Design,do%20you%20push%20through%20that%3F

Reuters. (2008, 04 22). Retrieved from https://www.reuters.com/article/us-boeing-airbus/boeing-airbus-agree-to-work-on-air-traffic-issues-idINWNAS879720080422

Ross, L., & Naoum, K. (2023, 05 05). Retrieved from https://www.thomasnet.com/insights/apple-supply-chain/

Sheridan, D. (2010, 02). Retrieved from https://medium.com/fact-of-the-day-1/october-5-salesforces-1-1-1-model-b86a13625b6c

Sherry, B. (2022, 10 21). Retrieved from https://www.inc.com/ben-sherry/michael-dubin-dollar-shave-club.html

Shih, W. C. (2022, 10 15). Retrieved from
        https://hbr.org/2022/11/what-really-makes-toyotas-
        production-system-resilient
Simmons University. (n.d.). Retrieved from
        https://pocketsights.com/tours/place/John-Quelch%3A-the-
        Pirate-Captain-Killed-by-His-Fortune-29087:3643
Simon, D. R. (2022, 01 19). Retrieved from
        https://www.historyextra.com/period/stuart/anne-bonny-
        mary-read-female-pirates-lives-crimes/
Smedra, J. (2022, 06 20). Retrieved from
        https://www.savingadvice.com/articles/2022/06/20/1095938
        _costco-keeps-employees-happy.html
Smith, S. (2020, 06 25). Retrieved from
        https://www.investors.com/news/management/leaders-and-
        success/jack-dorsey-changed-the-world-twice-twitter-square/
Soni, S. (2015, 22 09). Retrieved from www.entrepreneur.com:
        https://www.entrepreneur.com/en-in/business-news/meet-
        oyo-rooms-founder-ritesh-agarwal-the-indian/250907
Southwest Airlines. (2015, 10 08). Retrieved from
        https://www.prnewswire.com/news-releases/southwest-
        airlines-brings-transfarency-to-airline-industry-
        300156533.html
Souza, K. (2021, 12 01). Retrieved from
        https://talkbusiness.net/2021/12/walmart-supply-chain-and-
        logistics-chief-talks-about-challenges-lessons-learned/
Starbucks. (2020, 02 28). Retrieved from
        https://stories.starbucks.com/press/2020/cafe-practices-
        starbucks-approach-to-ethically-sourcing-coffee/
Sullivan, M. (2017, 06 20). Retrieved from
        https://www.fastcompany.com/40433541/apples-obsession-
        with-secrecy-may-be-a-self-fulfilling-prophecy
Tabrizi, B. (2023, 02 20). Retrieved from
        https://hbr.org/2023/02/how-microsoft-became-innovative-
        again

thewayofthepirates.com. (n.d.). Retrieved from
http://www.thewayofthepirates.com/:
http://www.thewayofthepirates.com/famous-
pirates/bartholomew-roberts/

Thompson, A. (2018, 12 30). Retrieved from
https://www.wired.com/story/this-year-spacex-made-us-all-
believe-in-reusable-rockets/

Verge. (2018, 09 27). Retrieved from
https://www.theverge.com/2018/9/5/17823490/google-
20th-birthday-anniversary-history-milestones

Wikipedia. (n.d.). Retrieved from
https://en.wikipedia.org/wiki/Samuel_Bellamy

Wikipedia. (n.d.). Retrieved from
https://en.wikipedia.org/wiki/Anne_Dieu-le-Veut

Wikipedia. (n.d.). Retrieved from
https://en.wikipedia.org/wiki/Pirate_code

Wikipedia. (n.d.). Retrieved from
https://en.wikipedia.org/wiki/Governance_in_18th-
century_piracy

Wilson, G. (2021, 06 28). Retrieved from
https://manufacturingdigital.com/lean-manufacturing/lego-
expands-its-sustainable-manufacturing-practices

Wolfe, I. (2023, 03 29). Retrieved from https://goodonyou.eco/how-
ethical-is-patagonia/

Zubrow, K. (2023, 04 16). *www.cbsnews.com*. Retrieved from
https://www.cbsnews.com/news/how-googles-dont-be-evil-
motto-has-evolved-for-ai-age-60-minutes-2023-04-
16/#:~:text=When%20Google%20filed%20for%20its,in%20Go
ogle's%20code%20of%20conduct.